REVIVAL

A Study in Biblical Patterns

by

David Boyd Long

ISBN 0-946351-38-4

Copyright 1993 by John Ritchie Ltd.
40 Beansburn, Kilmarnock, Scotland

Typeset by Newtext Composition Ltd., Glasgow
Printed by Bell and Bain Ltd., Glasgow

Foreword

THE apostle Paul in his epistles records an extensive list of beloved fellow-workers with whom he had laboured in the work of the gospel and church-planting. There was Luke the beloved physician, Timothy his son in the faith, and Titus the Christian diplomat etc. One of the great blessings of a servant of God is to have faithful and loyal fellow-workers to share with him in times of stress and difficulty.

I esteem it an honour and a privilege to be invited to write a brief foreword to the book of my esteemed brother and fellow-labourer David B. Long on the theme of *Patterns of Revival*. I have carefully read the manuscript and am thankful for the thorough research into the history of the subject of revival in the OT scriptures.

This book makes a distinction between abortive and genuine revival. Genuine revival is characterised by the following features:

It is the work of the sovereign Spirit of God.

It commences with true repentance, confession and abandonment of sin.

It involves strict adherence and obedience to the word of God.

I have heard some of the chapters of this book expounded in the public ministry of brother David Long and am glad that they are now available in this permanent form. It is my earnest prayer that it may be used of God for His glory and for the blessing of His dear people.

T. E. Wilson

Dedicated
to

The Head of the Church
and all the members of His Body,
and to "Jedidah"
who was always there

Preface

THIS little book is written in plain words for plain Christians confused by the many programmes for revival with which they are being confronted.

For this reason there are quite a few things the reader will not find here.

"There are no quotations from learned authors, no impressive theological or philosophical terms, and no lengthy bibliography. Of course quite a few books have been read in a long lifetime, and all that has been learned from godly writers of the past is gratefully and humbly acknowledged.

Another reason for the absence of a bibliography is the fact that we are not dealing with any of the revivals outside Biblical times and records. We sincerely thank God for all such revivals, most of which have been dealt with by far abler pens than ours. This, very simply, is not our aim.

Our aim has been to lead the Christian seeking patterns for revival directly to the Sacred Writings themselves, where such events have been recorded by God the Holy Spirit with His own interpretations and applications.

Spiritual revival is, by definition, spiritual. This clearly means that it is brought about in our spirits by God's Spirit, and is therefore quite distinct from merely external or organisational change. Returning to God to find spiritual restoration may well bring about many much needed changes in how we do things, as well as in the results obtained. We must not, however, confuse cause with effect, or mistake change for revival. We could make all the outward changes imaginable or desired, many of them perhaps good and even necessary, and still be in heart as far away from God as ever.

With deep humility, therefore, and a very real sense of inadequacy and imperfection, we commend this simple study to God and His people, praying that He may in His grace be pleased to bless it for His own glory.

Ballygowan,
N. Ireland, 1992

Table of Contents

                                                              Page
Chapter 1. Introduction 1
         2. Revival under Joshua 9
         3. Disobedience and Defeat in Judges 14
         4. Revival under Samuel 28
         5. Revival under David.....................................35
         6. Solomon and the Division of the Kingdom ...38
         7. Revival under Hezekiah:
            Preparation by God.....................................45
         8. Revival under Hezekiah: Its Execution 51
         9. Revival under Hezekiah: Its Results..............63
        10. Revival under Hezekiah:
            Satanic Opposition 75
        11. After Hezekiah: Losing Ground...................78
        12. Revival under Josiah: Its Beginnings 84
        13. Revival under Josiah:
            Rediscovery of the Scriptures........................90
        14. Josiah: The Results of Finding the Book 98
        15. Back from Babylon 102
        16. Revival of the Exile: A Divine Work............110
        17. Revival after the Exile:
            Laying the Foundation................................117
        18. Revival after the Exile: Enemies in Action ..120
        19. Revival after the Exile: The Second Stage ..128
        20. Revival after the Exile:
            Restoration to the Land 132
        21. Revival after the Exile:
            Problems in the Land................................138
        22. Revival after the Exile:
            The Great National Bible Reading 142

23. Revival after the Exile:
    Nehemiah's Opponents 147
24. Revival after the Exile:
    The Word Acknowledged 152
25. Revival after the Exile:
    The Model Messenger 154
26. An Abortive Revival under Asa 157
27. An Abortive Revival under Jehoshaphat 162
28. An Abortive Revival under Joash 174
29. Conclusions 177

1

Introduction

1. Introductory Questions

THIS book attempts to answer humbly four questions regarding the much discussed subject of spiritual revival:

1. Is there a record of revivals in Scripture?
2. If there is such do they show a clear and consistent pattern?
3. What is that pattern?
4. Is the pattern relevant and practicable in our day?

That there are such revivals would be hard to deny. Those in the days of Hezekiah and Josiah, kings of Judah, and later at the return from Babylon in the days of Ezra and Nehemiah, are known and acknowledged by all serious Bible readers. Less frequently recognised but nonetheless real are those under Joshua and Samuel, and in every instance the pattern is clear and described in detail. There are also at least three others under kings Asa, Jehoshaphat and Jehoash, which began with promise but petered out in failure. It is our belief that the study of these failed revivals is also important if we are to avoid the mistakes that marred them, and we intend to devote some study to them later in the book.

2. Present Day Need For Revival

The need for revival in our day is too obvious to be denied and there are many burdened hearts among Christians everywhere about spiritual conditions. There is genuine concern about the apathy, worldliness, and resultant lack of effectiveness in our testimony. Some mourn the poor quality of worship and teaching among us. Others are more occupied with the lack of bold and Biblical preaching of the Gospel in clarity, conviction, and power, and a lack of genuine conversions proved by radically changed lives.

Some see the above features as merely the surface and visible results of a deeper spiritual cause, namely, lack not only of heart affection for Christ, but also of devotion to Him and obedience to His word. This, at least in part, they attribute to the inroads of materialism, carelessness of walk, lack of personal holiness, and a general conformity to the thinking and lifestyle of the society around us.

Others seem to focus more on the need for growth in numbers, activity and zeal in service, success in winning converts. Whatever the approach there can be no doubt about the need for revival, and to this we shall address ourselves.

3. Terminology used

Different words are used for the experience with which we are dealing. The word we are using, and which has been used throughout generations from Bible times is "revival" with its verb form "to revive". The Oxford Dictionary, among other things outside our subject, defines the word as: "to bring back to life, vigour, activity etc". The noun in a religious sense is given as "efforts to promote reawakening of religious fervour". It is the term most frequently used in the Bible. The heart cry "Wilt thou not revive us again?" in Ps 85:6 says it all.

"Renewal" has become more popular with some in recent times, and is also a perfectly good word, also used in the Bible, though less frequently. It is noticeable that in the Bible in this connection it is consistently used for something very inward and personally spiritual rather than outward or structural. In Ps 51:10, especially in the context of David's recovery from a serious spiritual fall, the words "renew a right spirit within me" show this clearly. In Isa 40 the promise of renewal of strength is personal and dependent on "waiting on the Lord". In Lam 5, "Renew our days" is a cry for national restoration after the destruction of Jerusalem. In 1 Sam 11:14 the "kingdom is renewed" in the sense of allegiance being declared. In the NT we have "the inward man renewed" (2 Cor 4:16); the "new man renewed in knowledge" (Col 3:10); "renewing of the mind" (Rom 12:2; Eph 4:23); "regeneration and renewing by the Holy Spirit", that is in new birth (Titus 3:5).

Other words such as restoration and refreshing are used. We use the word "revival" not because it is intrinsically more correct, but because it has been so widely used, is clearly understood, and seems free from any slant or particular association. Renewal has been used in a quite different sense by the Roman church, as well as various "kingdom", "charismatic", and "house church" movements, not to mention cults; such associations we would prefer to avoid.

4. The Causes of Revival

Of suggested ways for achieving this desired end there is great variety. Some refer to "praying down revival", apparently feeling that revival comes when we desire it enough and pray with sufficient earnestness for it. Others say that it happens spontaneously, from the sovereign grace of God, often without discernable cause or circumstance. No doubt there is truth in both these views since earnest prayer would indicate a sense of need, perhaps a much needed repentance, and God does answer prayer. We must also recognise that, whatever the circumstances, all spiritual help or activity comes from God and therefore is dependent on His sovereignty and grace. It seems to this writer, however, that both views leave something out.

Still others seem to be saying that the cure for our ills, and the way to deal with the aforementioned problems, so evident among us, is through theologically-trained leaders who would provide a better quality of public ministry which, in turn, would bring in greater numbers of people.

This, we are told, calls for reorganisation and restructuring of public services, and use of seminaries. Many suggest that having a man in charge of each local church would solve, or help solve, the problems, provided we set goals such as so many people to be converted and numbers to be increased by a specified percentage over a predetermined period.

These examples should suffice to illustrate the variety of viewpoints, even confusions, which prevail, and so we turn to the certainties of Holy Scripture itself.

a. Revival In the New Testament

The NT has recorded relatively little history, and since that little deals mainly with the very earliest days it does not describe the experience of revival such as we find in the lengthy and detailed history of the OT. There are, however, quite a few hints and important principles to be found, and they merit our careful attention.

i. A NT example: Acts 20:17-38

In this passage the apostle Paul called the overseers of the church at Ephesus to meet him at Miletum. He there addressed them in the most solemn terms about the danger of departure in days to come. The departure, it must be emphasised, was not from rules or structures developed by men, but from apostolic teaching inspired by God. The danger would come in two main forms: first, from heretical teachers ("wolves") from the outside who would ravage the flock, and second, from men from among their own number (the overseers) who would teach perversions of the truth. By means of warped interpretations of truth, this second group would divide and sectionalise the Christians, leading disciples after themselves.

This is clearly a prophetic picture of departure from original patterns, and the question is: Did the apostle give directions as to how to guard against this before it happened, or how to regain original conditions after it took place? The answer is not far to seek. First he reminds them

of the pattern of his work among them in the very earliest
days, and this can be summed up in the one word
"teaching" (of the Scriptures). He reminds them that he
kept back nothing profitable to them, declaring, teaching,
testifying. He then charges these overseers that in turn they
"feed the church of God" in view of the approaching evil.
This is obviously given as the only cure.

Again in v. 32 he emphasises the value of teaching as he
concludes his message: "And now brethren, I commend you
to God and to the word of His grace which is able to build
you up and give you an inheritance with all them which are
sanctified". Neither the apostle, nor the divinely-inspired
writer, suggests any philosophies of ministry,
reorganisations or restructurings; no sending of promising
men to Antioch or Jerusalem for more advanced theological
training; no suggestion that the elders might be too old or
old-fashioned and so should move over to make way for a
younger and better educated generation. There is offered
no quick and painless solution, no short cut. It is simply
"God and the word of His grace", taught, accepted,
submitted to, and obeyed.

ii A NT example: 1 Timothy 4

In 1 Tim 4, the whole of which merits careful reading
and thought, Paul predicts the appearance in later times of
trouble and error which come basically from "departing
from the faith". "The faith" clearly means the divine
revelation on which our faith rests, as in Jude 3; Phil 1:27
and many other passages. Departing from this is not
setting aside some mere human tradition or dogma but,
among other things, departure from the divine will and
intention. Those referred to are teachers and therefore to
be seen as operating within the fellowship of the professing
church, yet they are peddling teachings emanating from
demonic sources and accepted through "giving heed to
seducing spirits". The picture is a frightening one. In Ephes
2 those who are disobedient to the Gospel become those in

whom the prince of the power of the air works (effectively), and here in 1 Timothy any professing believer, even one with the standing of a teacher, who wilfully departs from the written revelation, is in equally grave danger.

The antidote is clearly spelled out. Timothy will be a good servant of Jesus Christ if he puts the brethren in remembrance of the instructions just given. "These things command and teach" refers to the same previously-written instructions, (v. 11); then, like a relentless hammering come the words: "Give attention to reading, exhortation, teaching . . . neglect not the gift that is in thee . . . meditate on these things, give thyself wholly to them . . . take heed to thyself and to the teaching for in so doing thou shalt both save thyself (as a teacher, from mistakes) and them that hear thee" (those taught, from being deceived). Surely the danger and the remedy could not be put in stronger terms. The message is that at all times, but particularly in times of spiritual threat, the most important bulwark is constant teaching of *the Word,* and total obedience to it.

iii A NT example: 2 Timothy 4

There are many more similar examples in the letters to Timothy but to avoid tediousness reference is made only to this one further passage. Here again we are warned that in days to come, *i.e.* after the apostolic era, the Lord's people would be in such a state that they would not put up with sound or healthful teaching. According to their own desires, they would seek out, the passage tells us, teachers who could titillate their jaded tastes with newer and fancier things, better suited to their styles and pretensions. The only cure suggested for the whole sad situation is "the word", heralded forth at every suitable opportunity: "with all diligence, reprove, rebuke, exhort, with all long-suffering and *teaching.*" Strong words indeed, and it is to be feared that in our day any rebuke or reproof would be labelled as uncharitable, unkind, or even unchristian.

iv A NT example: Revelation 3

The epistles of Peter, James, John and Jude, all written with end times in view, have much of the same thing, and are all worthy of careful consideration. But we close this section with a glance at the church in Laodicea in Rev 3:14. This arrogant and self-satisfied assembly, saturated with the spirit of humanism, was in sad condition in that it saw itself as needing nothing and able to handle its own problems. It was lukewarm — neither cold nor hot — which simply means that without an influence outside itself it had adjusted to the temperature of the surrounding pagan society. It was no different from the world around it. A comfortable sameness marked Laodicea; it had none of the healthy tang of salt nor the illuminating and revealing blaze of divine light. At the same time there was in this conceited congregation a shocking ignorance and unawareness of its own wretchedness, misery, poverty, blindness and nakedness or shame before the world. It is a classic example of an assembly in need of revival. Yet there is no instruction given regarding simple steps to this desired result. We find no word of programmes for brightening its meetings, improving its image, modernising its hymnology, getting better-class pulpit ministry, or a scheme for rejuvenating its elderhood. The cure must lie in the realm of the heart and spirit rather than in the outward and cosmetic. The cure is clearly spelled out. What they need must come from God, not from themselves or their own abilities. The prescription is:

> *Gold,* which throughout Scripture appears to stand for divine things, deity or, as in 1 Pet 1:7, the faith which lays hold of what is of God;
> *White Garments,* speaking of the righteousness of the saints as in Rev 19:8, a holy walk in testimony before God and men;
> *Eye Salve,* that they might see their condition, their need, and where and how that need might be met.

May these three not hint at Father, Son, and Holy Spirit, understood, enjoyed, and submitted to as true gain (gold), proper witness (white garments), with spiritual insight and power (eye salve)?

These passages and many others point to the Holy Scriptures studied, practised, taught, and obeyed as the only true defence against latter-day departure, and the only way back in revival and renewal.

b. Revival in the Old Testament

It also seems clear that the OT history of revivals emphasises precisely the same truth, and at this point it may be well to outline the direction of our study in these histories.

1. *Deuteronomy:* The foundation of all success and spiritual blessing is through obedience to God's Word.
2. *Joshua:* Revival after forty years of disastrous departure and backsliding.
3. *Judges:* Declension through disobedience and the calamitous results of this.
4. *1, 2 Samuel:* Revival under the first of the prophets, and its results into the reigns of David and Solomon.
5. *Kings and Chronicles:* Solomon's good start but later disobedience and departure with their consequences in division of the nation, idolatry, war, and self-destruction.
6. *Three Great Revivals* under Hezekiah, Josiah, Ezra and Nehemiah.
7. *Three failed revivals* which began with great promise under Asa, Jehoshaphat and Jehoash.

Chapter 2

Revival under Joshua

1. Before Joshua

IN order to understand something of the pattern of departure, failure, and revival in the OT we must have some very basic facts clearly in mind. Revival takes failure for granted, but since failure has been brought about by departure as we have suggested, then we have to ask the question: Departure from what? The answer to this lies at the very root of our study. The departure of which the Scriptures speak, and with which we are dealing, was not simply a leaving of the path of human wisdom or good sense. Nor was it merely the abandoning of the ways of their forefathers. It was something infinitely more frightening and reprehensible. It was a deliberate refusal to obey the written revelation of will and word of their Redeemer-God, a word to which they had pledged themselves with solemn vows.

When God brought His redeemed people out of Egypt He made a covenant with them at Sinai. In Exod 19 the basis of that covenant was laid out in the clearest of terms when God said: "If ye will obey my voice indeed, and keep my covenant, then ye shall be . . .". Moses brought this proposed contract down to the people who accepted it with the words: "All that the Lord hath spoken we will do" (vv. 5-8). The word given them was divided into three section marked by distinguishing titles.

"The *commandments*" referred to the individual and personal life of holiness which was necessary if blessing and communion with the God of holiness were to be enjoyed. These commandments were given in Exod 20: 1-26.

"The *judgments*" governed all relationships in the social

life, and are outlined in Exod 21:1-24:11.

"The *ordinances*" governed the religious life and are found in Exod 24:12-31:18.

Thus the whole life of this redeemed people was to be controlled and ordered by the word of God in every sphere and at every level. No other god was to usurp the Lord's place of primacy and uniqueness. No other word or rule could be obeyed or followed without incurring His displeasure and judgment. The books of Exodus, Leviticus and Numbers simply teem with warnings against any kind of departure from God's word even in the details of the materials and construction of His sanctuary, as well as in all service to and for Himself. This is an important point to remember.

"Deuteronomy" means "The Second Law", but this does not mean that it was an addition to what they already had. It was a review of what God had said earlier, and the reason for this is not far to seek. Those addressed were a new generation whose fathers had rebelled because of unbelief at Kadesh-Barnea (Num 13, 14). This new generation had wandered in the wilderness for forty years or had been born there during that time. All those who had disobeyed God's word died. Now, after the wanderings, the new generation had to be reminded of the importance of obedience to the word of God. They were near the crossing of Jordan, by the brook Arnon in the land of Moab (Deut 4:46-48), and a halt is called while the whole solemn business of reviewing the words of the covenant is undertaken. This was to be done again by order of Moses to Joshua when they actually entered the land, as recorded in Deut 27. That order was carried out by Joshua in 8:31 of his book, between the twin hills of Ebal and Gerizim with the blessing for obedience and the curse for disobedience being echoed by the priests as the whole text was read. We are told that "there was not a word" left out of the reading. What an impression this must have made! They were then made the custodians of this written contract between them and their God; it was carried by them inside the ark throughout their journeys, which is why the ark was called the ark of the covenant. See Exod 25-16; 40-20; Deut 10:2; Heb 9:4.

Furthermore Moses, by direct order from God, called Joshua before all the people as his successor, with a solemn charge of complete obedience to the words of the covenant.

2. Under Joshua

Rarely is the period covered by the book of Joshua recognised as one of revival, yet even a quick reading of the book will put the matter beyond doubt. This same people at Kadesh-Barnea, when within a few miles of the borders of the promised land, doubted God's ability to bring them in and refused to obey His word when ordered to go forward. Accepting the report of a ten to two majority, thus showing more confidence in human reasoning and planning than in the pledged and written word of God, they proposed returning to Egypt. When Moses, Aaron, Caleb, and Joshua begged them not to rebel they threatened stoning so that they could elect new leaders more to their liking to guide them back. For this they would be doomed to wander for those forty years until all that generation of a responsible age died. What a picture of failure, and what a need for revival.

The chapters preceding this collapse in Num 13 give us a classic picture of the downward steps that led to the breakdown. The needed revival was to be brought about by Joshua after forty years of wandering, barrenness and frustration, punctuated by the revolt of Korah and his clan and the consequent destruction of almost 15,000 people, the visitation of fiery serpents on murmurers and the harlotry of Baal-Peor. Thereafter according to Deut 31:7, God presented Joshua to the people as we have already mentioned, and delivered the word of God to them as the basis of all blessing and prosperity.

It may be well to pause at this point and make one thing clear. Some may think from what we have written that we see the Christian to-day as under the Law as were the Israelites. We have no such thought.

Although not under Law, Christians can learn from Israel's history. What Isreal was given was the word of God in which they were to trust without leaning on their own understanding. It was full of promises as well as guidelines; it revealed pledges of God's love, His care, His power and the immutability of His purposes for them. It also reminded them that only in obedience to His Word was there blessing: disobedience to it, or deviation from it, could bring only loss and disaster. It insisted that their God must be everything to them, enthroned in their hearts and in their lives. Every one of these statements can be shown to be as real to us in the NT era as to them in the Old.We can expect no blessing apart from obedience to God's word, and when we stray from it there is no path to restoration or revival apart from a return to that Word. We admit this when we sing the simple hymn:

Trust and obey, for there's no other way
To be happy in Jesus, but to trust and obey.

It is to be feared, however, that we sing the words with little attention to their meaning or implications.

In the first chapter of his book we are struck by God's charge to Joshua. We have the promise of God's power with him in the carrying out of the divine purposes, and the list of assurances is in blazing contrast to the preceding years of defeat and backsliding. At Kadesh-Barnea the human reasoning had been: the people (enemies) are too tall and strong, their cities are too heavily fortified and we are too weak. God and His word had no place in their assessment, and they were not ready to trust Him, despite Joshua and Caleb assuring that, "If the Lord delight in us then He will bring us into this land, and give it to us."

Now God's word to Joshua contained the following:
"Every place the sole of your foot shall tread upon, to you I
have given it." Note the past tense; in God's view the land
was already theirs.

And God added: "There shall not any man be able to
stand before thee all the days of thy life. I will not fail thee
nor forsake thee. Observe to do according to all the law,
which Moses my servant commanded thee. Turn not from
it to the right hand or the left that thou mayest have good
success wherever thou goest. This book of the law shall not
depart out of thy mouth (this refers to his teaching, as the
previous one did to his personal life and service), but thou
shalt meditate therein day and night that thou mayest
observe to do according to all that is written therein, for
then thou shalt make thy way prosperous, and then thou
shalt have good success . . .. For the Lord thy God is with
thee." In obedience to the Word, Joshua would have divine
support, for God cannot go with us in disobedience to His
word.

That Joshua "followed" both fully and faithfully is
affirmed at his death (Josh 24:31) in these striking words:
"Israel served the Lord all the days of Joshua, and all the
days of the elders who outlived Joshua and who had known
all the works of the Lord that He had done for Israel." This
man's influence was so great upon what had been a
defeated, confused and wayward mob that it not only
lasted to the very end of his life but beyond that of a whole
generation, through the elders whom he had taught and
trained. It was indeed a powerful revival when we take into
consideration the fact that he was dealing with fourth
generation slaves who were possibly illiterate or at best
semi-literate, and that it took place under nomadic
conditions in a desert with no teaching helps or facilities of
any kind.

Chapter 3

Disobedience and Defeat in Judges

1. After Joshua

THE first one and a half chapters of Judges form a link with the happy days which marked the period of blessing immediately following Joshua's death and continuing into the days of his disciples and successors. It begins with unity, power and victory from Jerusalem south to the Negev, and to the whole of Gaza, Ashkelon and Ekron, the land of the Philistines. This last phrase shows the contrast with the dark days at the end of Judges when Isreal was in slavery to the very Philistines over whom they had once triumphed. After those first balmy days of success we see a growing weakness and failure on almost every hand, and to this we are given the key. Immediately after what we read regarding the period of victory under the power and influence of Joshua come the frightening words: "there arose another generation who knew not the Lord, nor yet the works he had done for Israel. And the children did evil in the sight of the Lord, and served Baalim. And they forsook the Lord, the God of their fathers, which brought them out of the land of Egypt, and followed other gods, of the gods of the peoples round about them" (Judges 2:10-15).

The phrase "the God of their fathers" is interesting and significant. What was good enough for their fathers was not acceptable to the newer generation who, now settled in the land and more educated and sophisticated, possibly thought themselves better able to develop new philosophies. These led them to accept in place of God's word something which was more current in the surrounding society. In due course, this led them into a head-on collision with God Himself. The temptation to do this is always with us as human beings, and even as Christians, when we get sufficiently away from God to ignore or disobey His word. Satan would take the believer's eyes and affections away from what pleases God, and set them on the path to numerical success and growth that is so highly esteemed in the world. And yet conformity to that world society is something against which the Christian is warned in Scripture.

It must be kept in mind that the world against which we are warned throughout the NT and with which we are to have neither friendship nor fellowship, according to 2 Cor 6:14-16; James 4:4; 1 John 2:15, is seen by God as lying, in its entirety, "in the wicked one". We ourselves speak of a social world as well as a political, an intellectual, a philosophical and a business world. The Bible makes it clear that there is also a religious world, which is far more likely to influence us in our Christian life and church activities than for example the social world; it is the religious world which the Christian is tempted to imitate, especially if its methods and structures seemed more successful.

A Bible illustration may explain what we are saying. Long before Israel wanted a king like the nations, or copied their military or political arrangements, or even their social lifestyles, they had begun to copy their religious practices, even before they worshipped their gods. We have only to look at the story of the golden calf at Sinai in Exod 32 to see this. They chafed at delay after Moses' six weeks' absence. Faith was replaced by reasoning: "As for this Moses . . . we know not what has become of him," and by sight. "They saw that Moses delayed" but had no eyes for the man above, hidden with God; they required action, expressed in the world, "Up, make gods which shall go before us." The word for "gods", *eohim,* is normally used for God Himself. In v. 4 they refer to this calf as *elohim* who brought them up out of

Egypt and in v. 1 they say, "He will go before us", both of which referred to what Jehovah Elohim had done. Even Aaron called for a "feast unto Jehovah" (v. 5), and they offered burnt and peace offerings as they had done to Jehovah Himself (Exod 24:4-5). They had forgotten the repeated injunction against making any graven image, yet it seems they were not so much forsaking their own God for some pagan deity but rather worshipping Him in the form of an image just as the nations around them worshipped their gods. It avoided waiting for God and the ensuing slowness; it produced immediate action and results, and it certainly generated lots of enthusiasm since they stripped off their clothes and started dancing. They were only doing to Jehovah what the surrounding religious people did to their gods, but it violated the plain word of God, and ended in shame, embarrassment, and the judgment of God.

In spite of God's anger and discipline, in their later history they reverted again and again to the same sort of thing. We shall see this in detail in the book of Judges as well as in the reigns of the kings from Solomon onwards when they "sacrified to the Lord in the high places." God had prohibited the offering of sacrifices anywhere except in the place where He had chosen to put His name, and throughout the OT, the "high places" are associated with some of the vilest and most corrupting of pagan practices in the worship of their gods. Israel was simply worshipping the true God in the ways in which the pagan nations around them worshipped theirs. Of course it developed into worshipping the pagan gods later, but it began more innocently with imitating the religious forms prevailing in the surrounding societies. Let us remember that.

It is quite clear from Scripture, however, that the people of God should not be guided or influenced by religious fashions of the world any more than by its fashions in other areas. We have one standard and one only: the Holy

Scriptures which are given "that the man of God may be perfect, throughly furnished for every good work" (2 Tim 3:17). It is also important "that thou mightest know how thou oughtest to behave thyself in the house of God" (1 Tim 3:15). The same letter to Timothy warns us that we are to keep the sacred deposit, the word of God, and "avoid ... oppositions of knowledge falsely so called". Paul by the Holy Spirit sternly warned the early believers against "philosophies . . . after the traditions of men after (according to) the rudiments (or basic concepts) of the world, and not after Christ" (Col 2:8). In the same letter to Colosse we are reminded that since we have died to these rudiments of the world we should refuse to subject ourselves to them even though they may have a "show of wisdom". It should be fairly obvious from the context that these elements, rudiments and philosophies are religious in character.

It was in this very area that the sad departure recorded in the book of Judges began. Contrary to the orders of God "they made leagues" (reached suitable arrangements for co-operation) with the surrounding nations. Instead of demolishing the altars of false gods, they built their own: instead of following God and His word "they followed the gods of the people that were around them, serving Baal and Ashtaroth", basically the sun and moon gods of the heathen (Judges 2:11-13).

2. Patterns of Backsliding and Departure.

It is not our purpose to study all the sordid details recorded in the book of Judges, but rather to note as briefly as possible the roots of the whole history of failure and its main characteristics so that we might better understand the revival that followed in the days of Samuel. We are also told in 1 Cor 10 that the things that happened to Israel happened as picture lessons for us and are recorded for our warning that we should not fall into the same mistakes.

a. No Authority

First we note in Judges an almost total absence of references to the word of God, though in every earlier book of Scripture there is a constant repetition of such references, as also in the books of Samuel which follow. Even in the story of Ruth, which falls into the time of the Judges (but gives us a story of recovery and return), there are all sorts of direct and indirect references to God's word and ways; the phraseology of Ruth includes references such as finding grace, gleaning, the kinsman redeemer, the God of Israel under whose wings thou art come to take refuge, the acknowledging of a "nearer kinsman", acting before witnesses, the redeeming of the lost inheritance and of Ruth, the prayer and blessing of the people on Boaz and Ruth in their marriage.

But in Judges we are reminded four times (17:6; 18:1; 19:1; 21:25) that there was no king in the land, and since they had never had a king up to this time we must take this to mean that there was no authority, no central rule, no absolute standard. This is confirmed in two of the references by the addition of the words, "every man did that which was right in his own eyes". Human reasonings and philosphies had taken the place of the word of God, and we must remember that such philosophies are the very foundation of humanism, a way of thinking much more evident in Christian assemblies to-day than most are aware of. It is the concept that "we can do it", and it is also Laodiceanism — we have the potential and need nothing.

b. No Repentance

The second notable feature of this sad book is an absence of any turning to God in repentance on the part of the people as a whole. In the return from Babylon under Nehemiah, which we shall study later, the people gather themselves together as one man and ask Ezra to "bring the book". When he opened the book, they stood up in reverence, bowed down in humility and worship, and when it was read they cried "Amen!" and "all the people wept". In 1 Sam 7:2 we read that "they lamented after the Lord". There is nothing of this desire after God and His word in Judges. Indeed, apart from a few references to specific messages from God to individuals we find no mention of the Scriptures in the whole book. There is much mourning and sorrow because of defeat and bondage and also a seeking for deliverers, but no recorded repentance.

c. No Revival

While in the mercy of God there are many deliverers and deliverances in Judges, one looks in vain for any sort of spiritual revival. We read in 2:4 that when God rebuked them for their idolatry and sin they wept, but there is no sign of turning to Him for forgiveness and restoration. Instead there is steady deterioration. They begin in weakness, disorder, defeat, and turning to the gods of the nations for help, but they end in rank idolatry followed in the later chapters by a disgusting quagmire of harlotry, concubinage, sodomy, rape, murder and civil war with the almost total extermination of the tribe of Benjamin and forty thousand of the rest of Israel.

d. Deterioration in Leadership

The deterioration mentioned above was not only among the rank and file but very noticeable in the quality of the leaders. There is a vast difference between Othniel at the beginning and Samson at the end. The latter wreaked havoc on the Philistines but never associated the people with himself in it. He "judged Israel" for twenty years, but died in slavery himself and left the people in the same state; indeed in 15:11 they chide with him for trying to change their state and beg him to desist with the pathetic words: "Knowest thou not that the Philistines are rulers over us? . . . We have come to bind thee . . . to deliver thee into their hands". And what can be said of Ibzan, Elon, Abdon, Tola, and Zair? Few remember their names or their existence and all that is written of them seems only to accentuate their smallness and lack of any distinction. Of one it is only recorded that he had thirty sons and thirty daughters, marrying his daughters "abroad" and taking wives for his sons "abroad"; of others simply that after judging for certain years they died and were buried. Another had forty sons and thirty nephews who rode on seventy donkeys and he also died and was buried. Surely the very depths of abject mediocrity. How different from the regret of Heb 11: "the time would fail me to tell" of all the heroes of faith. We are also repeatedly reminded that when the judge or deliverer died the people promptly returned to their old ways and ended in their old defeat and subjugation. They wanted wanted a change without being changed themselves. How like us!

e. Wanted, a Man for Deliverance

Again and again in this book we find the people, when in difficulties, showing a rather pathetic hankering for a "man", instead of turning to God. It is interesting to note that while in the twenty-four chapters of Joshua we find the word "man" some twenty-five times, in the twenty-one chapters of Judges the word occurs one hundred and seven times. God, of course, uses men, and in His grace He raises up His men for special times of trouble and need, but it is more a people's dependence on a man and always looking for one to solve their problems that strikes one throughout this period. It seems, indeed, that as time goes on this tendency increases.

One or two illustrations will serve to make the point. In 10:18 we read: "What man is he who will begin to fight against the children of Ammon? He shall be head over all the inhabitants of Gilead." In other words, if he would take them out of their difficulty they would give him a permanent job as their leader. Leadership was popular in that day too. They got a man, and for a time it seemed to work, but it wound up with the man, Jephtha, leading them out to fight their brethren of Ephraim at a cost of 42,000 dead (12:4-6).

f. Wanted, a Man for Leadership

In chs. 6–8 we have the story of Gideon, a mighty man of God, as indeed was Jephtha.

Israel had done evil and as a result "The Lord delivered them into the hand of Midian seven years". Sometimes when we go to the world or its ways for help, the judgment of God is in leaving us there. They were in acute distress, hiding in dens and caves with neither courage nor capacity to help themselves (v. 2). Their country was virtually taken over by Midian and Amalek who devoured the crops, grazed their livestock on Israel's pastures, and left God's people "greatly impoverished", and "brought very low", words that would describe the condition of many an assembly if we are honest with ourselves.

After seven years of this they cried to the Lord, though there is no record of any repentance or change of heart, since we learn from v. 30 that when the deliverer, on orders from God, destroyed an idol which belonged to his own father, the local people demanded that he be brought out for lynching! In spite of this God in mercy gave deliverance by Gideon, and when they saw that by him they obtained release from the oppression of their enemies they wanted to make him king, and to establish a hereditary monarchy descending to his offspring (8:22). And this was the man they had wished to execute a short time earlier! Gideon wisely rejected such an arrangement, though they did not give up, since later they took his illegitimate son to rule over them. They had acquired an appetite for "a man".

g. The Leader's Failure

Though Gideon refused the kingship he was guilty of as great a mistake, for Satan does not give up easily either. Gideon asked for, and received, a great share of the plunder taken from the Ishmaelites and Midianites, including between sixty and seventy pounds weight of gold as well as jewels and costly purple fabric taken from the enemy kings. With these things he made an ephod which he installed in his own home town of Ophrah in Manasseh. All kinds of reasons have been put forward for the making of this ephod, any of which may be defended but not one of which can be proved. No matter which explanation we take, the whole business was an indefensible and wilful act of disobedience. The people soon came to treat this ephod with superstitious worship and it became a snare not only to them but to Gideon and his household. It is surely unthinkable that a man of Gideon's spiritual perception and godly fear, as shown in ch. 6, would have deliberately made the ephod as an idol, but his intention, however good, could not keep it from becoming one, something worthy of thought in our own day.

The whole nation was in disorder, confusion, and ignorance. There is no reference at all to a high priest, until we come to 1 Sam 1, "in the time of the Judges" and then the high priest is Eli, blind, both physically and spiritually, powerless to deal with evil in the Lord's house, and who has lost all contact with God since there is "no open vision, and the word of the Lord was precious (scarce)." There is therefore no understanding in Judges of priesthood, as we see from ch. 17 where Micah makes his son a priest with an ephod, in charge of his collection of idols, and later installs a Levite from Judah as his salaried priest. Was Gideon rash enough to wish to install himself as a priest though of the tribe of Manasseh? And if so did he imagine that all he needed was an ephod made of Ishmaelitish gold and totally unrecognised by God? Did he hope to receive messages and guidance through a homemade Urim and Thummim? Whatever may have been his motive, his work of art became an idol and the centre of idolatry.

As has already been pointed out there seems to have been nothing learned by the people from all this, not even from the fact that Gideon had refused the place of sole leader or king. We read that he had a multitude of sons by his "many wives" and one, son of a concubine, whom they made king, established a brutal dictatorship which began in the blood of his seventy half-brothers and ended in his own.

There is a plain lesson for us in all of this, as well as a parallel to much in our own days. There seems to be a tendency on the part of many to look for help, deliverance, or revival from others, or even to seek out some man on whose shoulders could be placed the responsibility for doing what we are not prepared to do ourselves.

It is a costly thing to work out the salvation of the local testimony as the Spirit exhorted the Philippians so long ago (Phil 2:12). The context in that chapter is a Christ who emptied Himself in service to others and for the accomplishment of the will of the Father. In this path He did not clutch to Himself what was His by right. Paul in the same chapter speaks of his joy in being "poured out", of Timothy who unlike the many did not seek his own interests, but cared genuinely for the state of others, and of Epaphroditus who did not consider his own life in the service of others. It is this spirit that should move every member of the body of Christ, each one functioning "for the upbuilding of the whole" and not being so busy looking after his own interests that he seeks out someone else, whom he may even gladly "support", to do what he should be doing; read Eph 4:16.

Such human arrangement may seem to work but further down the road we may find we have only exchanged one problem for another. Not infrequently we make our ideas a sort of sacred cow, an idol, without which no one can hope for Biblical solutions. Indeed some of these schemes become so sacred that to question them is to invite ridicule and scorn. We have some of these things brought out in a startling way in the next example of this constant seeking for "a man". We have noted a man for deliverance and a man for king or leader, now we find a man for priest and the story is in ch 17.

h. Wanted, a Man for Priesthood.

The haunting and obsessive dependence on a man was not restricted to the social, military, and political spheres, but permeated the religious life as well. We have suggested that with increasing spiritual decline the general behaviour of the people becomes more bizarre, and attempts at solving their problems become not only less in line with God's directions but even less rational.

Judges 17 tells of a son stealing money from his mother, thus violating three commandments: the fifth, eighth and tenth. His mother makes light of this because she had saved the money to make two different kinds of idols, thus violating the first and second commandments, and by linking the name of "the Lord" with the whole business she violates the third. The idols are made and Micah (the son) puts them in his house of idols. He makes an ephod and consecrates one of his sons as priest though it would seem they were all of the tribe of Ephraim. Here appropriately we have one of the occurrences of the statement: "In those days there was no king in Israel: every man did that which was right in his own eyes". When God's authority is set aside or ignored, one opinion or philosophy is as good as another.

At this point "a young man" of Bethlehem-Judah comes along and stays with them as he is "looking for a place," something man in the flesh seems frequently to be doing. Micah makes the young man his priest over his idols, a neat and cosy arrangement whereby the nameless young man is given clothing, board and lodging, and an annual stipend in silver. One wonders what happened to Micah's son who had held the position previously; but then there is always competition in this field, and always the danger that others better prepared may also be looking for a place.

It is now also being suggested that we need to set up some

sort of "mechanism" or employment agency, though we would never call it this, for bringing those seeking a place into touch with those seeking a man. We have long made fun of others who used such methods for "filling the pulpit" yet now, to our shame, we seem to be toying with the same schemes.

At least one of Micah's sons was old enough to be his priest yet at this point the father asks the newly-arrived young man to be his "father" as well as priest. This seems a startling reversal of roles at first sight until we recall that in circles where it should be least expected we see young men brought in to be "leaders and teachers" of those who are old enough to be their fathers and in many cases born again before the young aspirants were born the first time.

In Judges 17, almost in the same breath, we are told that the young man "became as one of his sons". Would the much used word "dichotomy" be appropriate here? Or is it just confused thinking? Then the idolatrous Micah "consecrates" the nameless young man, and he becomes his priest, and the saddest part of all this sad story is Micah's exultant summing up: "Now I know that the Lord will do me good, seeing I have a Levite as my priest". This would be farcical, were it not so blasphemous. The Holy Spirit in sorrow interjects a summing-up of this tragi-comedy of both cause and effect, in one damning sentence which had been pronounced in v.6 and is now repeated: "There was no king in those days."

In the eyes of Micah he had everything in place and felt that with such arrangements he could expect the Lord to do him good; in other words he was on the road to success. As though God could, or would, bless what was so far from all He had taught His people in His word, and mixed up with gross idolatry.

The men of the tribe of Dan in the south sent out spies to search for a country weak enough to be attacked and taken over for tribal expansion according to Judges 18. They

came to Micah's town and somehow recognised the young
Levite and asked him some very probing questions: Who
brought you here? What are you doing here? What have
you got here? Questions these which would search all our
hearts. Accepting him as a real priest, for there was no
spiritual perception in any of this, they then required him
to ask counsel from God concerning their expedition, and
he of course told them that God would prosper them. They
found the country they wanted where the inhabitants were
completely at rest and where there was nobody with
authority, and nobody to put them to shame for anything
(RV), so they returned to their country and reported to
those who had sent them the good news of the easy victory
ahead. The armed warriors set off, came to Micah's house,
took all his idols, his ephod, and his wealth. Then finding
the young Levite standing around they offered him a better
job to come with them and be their priest. Being a hireling
in the first place, he accepted. Micah, when he complained,
was threatened with sudden death.

So much for the success of human arrangements when
they are contrary to God's word. And thus ended this
tragic story which might serve as a summary of the whole
book, teaching us that when we leave God's word, or ignore
it, one man's theories are as good, or as bad, as another's.
Our Lord, while on earth, promised that the Holy Spirit
would "Guide (us) into all truth" but, as has been pointed
out by another, once we step outside "the truth" we are on
our own and can no longer count on His guidance. It is in
and into the truth that He guides us.

3. A Blind Leader

The story of Samson, the last of the leaders of this book,
is a sad one for he dies bound, blind, defeated
dishonoured and in slavery, in which also he left the people
he was supposed to deliver. His downward story began with
disobeying God's word because what he wanted was right in
his own eyes, and he died without any eyes. So the lesson

for us from this book is that it is folly to suppose that we can work out deliverance from our present poor state by looking to "a man", or that we can achieve revival by disobeying or ignoring God's word.

Chapter 4

Revival Under Samuel

1. Eli's Priesthood

THE spiritual deterioration and disaster recorded in the book of Judges "for our warning" (1 Cor 10:11) reached its lowest point in the beginning of 1 Samuel, where all is spelled out in the clearest of terms. There was no spiritual perception, for even Hannah's anguished prayer was mistaken for drunkenness; no sense of shame, for even the high priest's sons forced sexual immorality on the women who came to worship. There was no power for discipline in the house of God; Eli might rebuke his sons, but failed to expel them as priests, even though they were corrupt and "knew not the Lord". There was no fear of God as even priests made light of God's sacrifices and ate what was for Him, while the high priest is said to have given honour to his sons rather than to God.

There was also no open vision from God, and the word of God was scarce since He had ceased to speak to those in such corruption and when He did give a message it was one of judgment and had to be given to the youth Samuel. There was a blind priesthood, and the lamp of God was going out in the Tabernacle; there was no ark for the Philistines had taken it, and when father and sons were slain, Eli's daughter-in-law dying in childbirth summed it up in the name of her son *Ichabod,* "There is no glory". Such is the picture of a defeated and demoralised people, all because of departure from the word of God.

We must remember, of course, that in the book of Ruth we have the story of a godly remnant in spite of general failure and backsliding in "the time of the judges". Heaven honours the names of Naomi, Boaz, Ruth and no doubt

28

countless others who will be known only "in that day", but
would include the godly women at the end of Ruth who
praised God for His ways and prayed for His blessing. It
was through them and not through any national strategy
that God established a royal line "after His own heart", and
through others in the same period He produced Samuel
who would lead the nation back to God. It is true that in an
hour of folly the people even then ran ahead of God and
chose Saul to be king in imitation of the surrounding
peoples (1 Sam 8:5), but God set him aside and David
continued Samuel's revival, probably instructed by him.

2. A Remnant

The mention of this word "remnant" calls for remark
since the concept of a faithful remnant in any age is today
treated by some with contempt and mockery. We have even
read that "the remnant mentality is a hindrance to
renewal", a statement which seems odd on the part of
theologians when we find the word no less than sixty-six
times in Ezra, Nehemiah and the prophets in this very
sense. The same Hebrew word is twelve times translated
"residue" and in the same sense of a faithful core within the
people of God in a time of failure. The word is used in Rom
11:4-5, with "a seed" (9:29) also being used in
the same sense of Israel in a future day. In Rev 2:24 amidst
the corruption of the church at Thyatira under the
influence of the woman Jezebel a special message is sent to
"the rest .. as many as have not this teaching". In 3:4 we
read, again amidst corruption, that the Lord says: "Thou
hast a few names in Sardis which have not defiled their
garments." These passages seem to be saying that in every
age, no matter how serious the departure, God is always
looking for those whose hearts are true to Him and His
word. The words of the very last writer of the OT confirm
the same truth: "Then they that feared the Lord spake
often one with another: and the Lord hearkened and heard
and a book of remembrance was written, for them that

feared the Lord and that thought on His name, and they shall be mine, saith the Lord . . .." (Mal 3:16). A reading of this little book shows the condition of the mainstream of the nation where few feared Him, or thought on His name. The word "thought" here has the sense of "to think highly of" or "to honour". It is also not hard to recognise that, some four hundred years after Malachi's time, we have in the beginning of the Gospels a faithful remnant represented by Zacharias, Elizabeth, Joseph, Mary, Simeon, Anna and the seeking men who became the Lord's first disciples, and no doubt there were many more. They shine with a heart-warming purity of faith against the disastrous background of the Maccabean period which collapsed in intrigue, corruption, murder and national defeat and shame.

3. Samuel's Influence

Samuel's great work was to bring Israel back from the sort of disaster and defeat seen at the end of Judges to the condition of the same nation under David. That failure was not due to lack of organisation, education or human ability. God put it clearly when He laid the charge: "You have not obeyed my voice" (Judges 2:2). Accordingly the revival under Samuel was not the result of any human strategy, but Samuel's work was to bring Israel back to the word of God and its obedience. In this he was successful, leaving the imprint of his teaching long after his death, as did Joshua. How beautiful that it should all begin with a broken and childless woman in her sadness for "a man child". She did not now merely crave to have a baby for her own satisfaction and to compete with Peninnah. She wanted a man, dedicated to God, who would bring Israel back under the authority of God's word and will. God answered her prayer for His own glory.

a. Samuel's First Lesson

The first step in the whole process had to be the

experience of being spoken to personally by God, for without this no man will accomplish anything for God. As is so often the case this happened at night, alone before the Lord in His house. It is the lesson of listening to God in a time of darkness, prepared to carry His message even when it is one of judgment, and therefore unpleasant, even dangerous. God's voice will never puff us up with notions of our ability or self-sufficiency, but will always show us His judgment against the sin of presumption as in the case of Eli's sons. In the end of ch. 3, as Samuel grew, the Lord was with him and confirmed His word in Samuel's mouth so that all Israel knew that he was established a prophet of the Lord, that is a mouthpiece for God. The pivotal statement is: "The Lord revealed Himself to Samuel in Shiloh by the word of the Lord" (1 Sam 3:21). This shows us clearly where all revival must begin.

b. The Pathway to Repentance

In chs. 4, 5, 6 the ark is lost and then brought back. It is the very emblem of God's presence among His people. Regarding the mercy-seat which covered it He had said: "There will I meet with you and will commune with you . . . of all things which I will give you in commandment . . .." When God communes with His people it will always be through His word and about His word. With the ark among them again in ch. 7, though not yet in its proper place, 7:2 tells us that "all Israel lamented after the Lord". As always God's presence is making them increasingly conscious of their failure. This is something totally absent in Judges where they begged for deliverance from their sorrows but never appear to have grieved over the lost presence of God. At this point Samuel calls them to a great conference at Mizpah and the challenge is put to them with the blunt words: "If ye do indeed turn to the Lord with all your hearts, then put away the foreign gods and Ashtaroth from among you and serve Him only and He will deliver you out of the hand of the Philistines", which is where the disobedience of Judges had left them. This the people willingly did, thus proving the genuineness of their repentance and sorrow, and though Satan attacked immediately in the form of the Philistines, a young lamb (precious thought) is brought, slain before God, and His people are delivered by direct divine intervention. The restoration was on its way, and the pathway to it is unmistakably clear.

c. Samuel's Teaching Ministry

The gathering at Mizpah was the beginning of blessing, a willingness to meet with God, to listen to His word, and to obey it, but Samuel knew that ignorance was as dangerous as disobedience, so he set himself the task of systematic instruction. This he accomplished by travelling every year in a circuit of four cities, including his own. Each one of these four places was significant in itself and would be well known to them as Hebrews for what had occurred there: *Bethel* ("the house of God") was no material house, but where Jacob had learned of the nearness of God; *Gilgal,* where circumcision had been renewed after years of negligence (that is the setting aside of the flesh, as useless, rejected by God) before Israel could go into the land of promise; *Mizpah,* where the Spirit came on Jephtha enabling him to win his great victory over Ammon; *Ramah,* near which Deborah dwelt under a palm tree giving Barak counsel which led to Israel's victory over Jabin, king of Canaan.

When Israel became determined to have a king like the other nations around, and possibly in view of the failure of Samuel's sons to follow his example of obedience, it became his sad duty to warn them against such a move as being really a rejection of the sovereignty and all-sufficiency of God. All the truth was laid before them. Samuel did not try to see what the majority wanted. He called their wish a rejection of God and warned of the consequences, some of which became evident very soon, others coming in later years. His job was to warn, and this he did before God.

Plain warning is not a pleasant job for the one who does it, and is often resented, misinterpreted, and on the whole is never a way to popularity. Yet much of the NT writing is taken up with warning (or admonishing which is the same thing). A younger generation of servants was charged to undertake the same ministry. Acts 20:31; 1 Cor 4:14; Col 1:28 show that Paul did this himself; Rom 15:14; 2 Thess 3:15 show that he urged others not to neglect such work. Titus was obviously expected to do it (Titus 3:10) and the word "to charge" carrying some of the same meaning was urged on Timothy in his ministry as well.

In dealing with king Saul, Samuel also had the unpleasant and dangerous task of teaching him, at least twice, sad and indeed tragic lessons about the seriousness of disobedience or even incomplete obedience. Parts of these stories are told us in 1 Sam 13:8-14; 15:9-23 respectively. In the first case Samuel's message is: "You have done foolishly, you have not kept the command of the Lord your God". In the second it is: "To obey is better than sacrifice . . . you have rejected the word of the Lord, he also has rejected you from being king". There is much profit in a full reading of both passages. We advise all to consider carefully the total failure and rejection by God of all that is done in disobedience of, or in partial obedience to, His word. Leaving out what is unpleasant to us, or what we may think unnecessary or even outdated is a seriously flawed response to God's will. In vain did Saul plead that he thought it was all right: in vain did he try to put the blame on "the people" (the good old standby of "consensus"). He was responsible as a leader and he paid an awesome price. Solemnly Samuel had warned Saul at his anointing and coronation: "If you obey His voice and do not rebel against the commandment of the Lord you . . . will continue . . . if you do not obey . . . but rebel against the command of the Lord then the Lord will be against you."

d. Samuel's Greatness

Four subsequent references to Samuel in Scripture give some idea of the work, character and stature of this man of God. In 2 Chron 35:18, speaking of the wonderful passover which marked the great revival under Josiah more than four hundred years after Samuel's death we read: "There was no passover like (it) kept in Israel from the days of Samuel the prophet". In Ps 99:6 we read: "Moses and Aaron among the priests and Samuel among them that call upon His name; they called on the name of the Lord and He answered them". Jer 15:1 says; "Though Moses and Samuel stood before me yet my mind could not be toward this people". In Hebrews the list of great leaders of the faith is capped with those of "David and Samuel". To be linked with such great men as Moses, Aaron, David and Josiah marks Samuel as outstanding, at least in God's eyes.

Chapter 5

Revival Under David

1. The Influence of Samuel

MUCH of Samuel's greatness was because of the far-reaching influence his ministry had on king David. Though David is not usually seen as having begun a great spiritual revival his name must ever be linked with Samuel who did, and we should probably think of him as being the learner under Samuel and the one who carried through what the prophet had begun. We have seen from the scriptures cited above that not only was Samuel's name mentioned in association with three of the OT's greatest men, Moses, Aaron and Josiah, but in the NT his name is directly linked with David's in the list of great men of the faith. Samuel anointed David as king and was most likely his mentor and guide during the troubled times of his rejection and persecution by Saul. This we gather from 1 Sam 19 when, in one of the darkest hours of this period David, under great strain, went to Ramah to consult Samuel, and the result was that the latter left his home and threw in his lot with the fugitive at Naioth. Under Samuel's influence David became "the man after God's own heart" and one of the most outstanding characters of the whole Bible. There are, in the Scriptures, in round numbers, 250 references to Abraham, 880 to Moses, and 1,200 to David.

It is also a fact that David's lifelong desire after God and His word, as well as obedience to that word, seen not only in his historical record but also in his psalms, is such that he set a standard by which all the succeeding kings were measured and evaluated. From the time of his son to the end of the monarchy how often we read that so-and-so "did what was right in the eyes of the Lord as did his father

David". In the same way we find the words repeated on the other side, so-and-so "did evil like the kings of Israel (or like Jeroboam) and did not walk after the ways of his father David." Of Josiah, who initiated the greatest revival of all on the eve of the final desolation of the land, it is said that he "walked in all the ways of his father David and turned not to the right hand or to the left". What an example, and what a heritage he left for succeeding generations over a period of about 400 years.

This is the more striking when we remember that the first three kings reigned for forty years each, the Biblical period of testing. The first, Saul, was consistently disobedient and self-willed. The third, Solomon, started well but, by departure from the word of God and violation of His strictest orders, reintroducing idolatry, he ruined his life and sowed the seeds of the division of the kingdom. The second, David, as we have noticed, yearned after God and His word, considering it more important to him than his daily food, and after the house of the Lord where he wished to dwell all his life. It is to be noted that when David spoke of the house of the Lord, as in Ps 23, he was not referring to heaven but the sanctuary. See also Ps 27:4: "One thing have I desired of the Lord, that will I seek after; that I may dwell in the house of the Lord all the days of my life, to behold the beauty of the Lord and to enquire in His temple." David's love for "the house of the Lord" echoes throughout his psalms. He was the man who thought of bringing the ark of the covenant back to Jerusalem. He was also the man who first wanted to make a temple for the Lord in the capital and, though not permitted by God to do this, he prepared much of the money and materials for it and charged his son Solomon with the actual work.

2. Supporting David

It is important for our study that we keep in mind also that David was not alone in the continuation of Samuel's work of revival. He had the support and guidance of three remarkable men of God: Nathan the prophet, Gad the seer and Zadok the priest. 1 Sam 19:20 tells of a great crowd of prophets around Samuel so he obviously gathered suitable men around him and trained them in the word of God. Where else would Nathan and Gad have obtained their training in the ways of God in view of the lack of anything of this sort in Judges? How much the king owed to these men we shall probably never know down here, but it is quite clear that he owed them much. Humanly speaking David owed to Nathan even his spiritual restoration. Some nine times we read of Gad's messages to David, several of these in times of great danger or distress. Through Samuel, Kings and Chronicles even a cursory reading of references to Zadok will make clear his immense influence throughout David's whole career. Neither did this priest's influence end with his life. Ezra, who was responsible for a great part of the revival at the return from Babylon is specifically traced as great-grandson of Hilkiah the priest who had a great part in the revival under Josiah, and he in turn was said to be the great-great-grandson of Zadok. Even in the dark days of Ezekiel God referred to: "The sons of Zadok that kept the charge of my sanctuary when the children of Israel went astray from me" (Ezek 44:15-16). As we consider other Scriptures and revivals we shall have cause to refer to these long connecting links of faithful ones across more than one generation or even one age. There is much to learn from these links.

Chapter 6

Solomon and the Division of the Kingdom

1 Kings 1-12 with 2 Chronicles 1-9

1. A Good Start

WE have seen the reign of David as one of great blessing, joy and expansion for Israel, accompanied as he was by Samuel, Gad, Nathan, Zadok and all his other "mighty men". This should have been a great example as well as a stimulus to his son Solomon who succeeded him on the throne. And few kings can have begun their reign with more promise than did Solomon, son of a father who was musician, poet, soldier, statesman, national hero and above all else, "the man after God's own heart". That father had honoured God's word, loved His house, and planned and provided for the building of a greater house. But apart from his upbringing, he had also before him the examples of Israel's first two kings, Saul and his own father. They were living lessons, so sharp, so clear, so powerful that they could neither be misunderstood nor ignored.

Disobedience to God's word had left Saul abandoned by God and man, a king powerless and put to shame, a warrior defeated, stripped, mutilated and, with his sons, nailed in scorn to the wall of Beth Shan, a fortress city in the heart of Israel and now the centre of Philistine power in the land. David, in spite of blunders into horrible sin, was essentially a man who was not only committed to obedience to God's law but one who loved that law and delighted in the house and ways of God. To him the law, statutes and ordinances of the Lord were "more to be desired than much fine gold and sweeter than honey" (Ps 19:10). "To dwell in the house

38

of the Lord always" was the condition nearest to his heart
(Ps 23:6). Solomon had these two reigns before him, each
one lasting forty years, as would his own.

He was brought in pomp on king David's royal mule to
the spring Gihon for anointing, coronation and
proclamation, surrounded by Zadok, Nathan and Benaiah,
symbols of David's power and success in the spiritual,
administrative and military spheres; see 1 Kings 1.

Then comes the solemn charge from David himself:
"Keep the charge of the Lord thy God, to walk in His ways,
to keep His statutes, His commands, His ordinances and
His testimonies as it is written in the law of Moses, that thou
mayest prosper ..." (1 Kings 2:1-4).

In ch. 3 of the same book, Solomon goes to Gibeon where
the Lord appeared to him, and there Solomon asked God
for "an understanding heart . . . that I may discern between
good and bad". Because he asked for this instead of
material blessings, God gave him both the understanding
and also riches and honour. To this the Lord added a
condition: "If thou wilt walk in my ways and keep my
statutes and my commandments as thy father David did,
then I will lengthen thy days". From that wonderful
experience the king returned to Jerusalem, stood before
the ark of the covenant of the Lord, and worshipped with
burnt offerings and peace offerings.

2. A Great Work

From that he proceeded to the immense job of building
what became known as Solomon's temple, but which in
reality was "the house of the Lord". Into this work he
poured his own wealth as well as that of the nation, along
with its finest craftsmen and artists and the whole labour
force. This was a soul-thrilling beginning for the new reign,
and one which promised great things for the future. The
glow of success was over it all. Immediately after the
consecration of the temple in ch. 8 God appeared to him "the
second time, as He had appeared to him at Gibeon" (9:2).

The words, as well as their order and emphasis, are intended to impress the solemnity of the scene upon the reader: "If thou wilt walk before me as David thy father, in integrity of heart and uprightness, to do according to all that I have commanded thee, and will keep my statutes and my judgments; then I will establish the throne of thy kingdom over Israel for ever . . . But if ye shall turn away from following me, . . . and not keep my commandments . . . but shall go and serve other gods . . . then will I cut off Israel out of the land which I have given them; and this house which I have hallowed for my name will I cast out of my sight and Israel shall be a proverb and a byword among all peoples." God was re-emphasising the previous warning. He saw what probably few, if any, humans saw, and the warning left Solomon without excuse for his future mistakes.

3. The Signs of Slippage

Immediately after this we notice some ominous signs of slipping: the giving away of twenty cities of a land already given by God to the tribes in trust, the multiplying of wealth, the strange incursion of Pharaoh into Israel to fight with Canaanites, the taking of Gezer for his daughter, Solomon's wife, the enlarging of territory and the making of the inhabitants into slaves and the heaping up of horses and chariots which God had prohibited and which probably came from Egypt. All these seem to bode little good for Solomon and Israel; especially ominous is the mention of an Egyptian wife, the daughter of Pharaoh. On the surface, however, all seemed well, with growth on every hand, prosperity in every sphere. The obvious plan of expansion was working well, involving armies, merchant fleets, and all the work projects within the nation itself. All this no doubt received high marks from most people in his own day and would perhaps even in ours since it seemed to be working and appeared to be a success. There was, however, another and more important view.

4. The Divine Evaluation of Solomon's Prosperity

In spite of all the activity and success in men's eyes, in 11:9 we find these heart-chilling words: "The Lord was angry with Solomon because his heart was turned from the Lord God of Israel . . . he kept not that which the Lord commanded". Sentence therefore was pronounced as follows: "Because thou hast not kept my covenant and my statutes I will surely tear the kingdom away from thee and will give it to thy servant (11:11). This was a severe judgment but it had been said before to king Saul in 1 Sam 15:22: "Has the Lord as great delight in burnt offerings and sacrifices as obeying the voice of God? To obey is better than sacrifice, and to hearken than the fat of rams". And in 1 Sam 13:13 to the same Saul is the warning: "Thou hast done foolishly, thou hast not kept the commandment of the Lord thy God . . . thy kingdom shall not continue". Note the almost identical words: "I will surely tear the kingdom from thee" and "thy kingdom shall not continue". The very thing each man was trying to save or strengthen, he destroyed by not obeying the word of the Lord. There is a warning here for us and for all ages.

We shall never succeed in strengthening or reviving anything spiritual by substituting our plans for God's word, no matter how good our plans appear to be, or how sincere we may be in our desires. Saul in one passage thought it a good thing to have a great sacrifice for God of Amalek's cattle, cattle God had ordered to be destroyed. He saved Agag himself whose execution God had ordered; perhaps he thought there was a chance of terminating Amalek's hostility, or of developing a strategy of peaceful accommodation. In the other passage he thought that because Samuel had not arrived on time there was nothing very wrong in trying to hold the crowds. He chose not to wait God's time and did what God had forbidden: he offered sacrifices which should only have been sacrificed on God's altar, and he invaded the priestly office belonging only to Aaron's family. Uzziah, a far better man than Saul, was smitten with leprosy for this very sin.

5. The Course of Departure

The first specific indication of departure is recorded in 1 Kings 3:1, even while the wonderful successes of this reign were still rolling forward, for we read: "Solomon made affinity (marriage alliance) with Pharaoh king of Egypt, and took Pharaoh's daughter and brought her into the city of David." We have evidence in 2 Chron 8:11 that Solomon was fully conscious of the wrong of this act when he said: "My wife shall not dwell in the house of David because the places to which the ark of the Lord has come are holy". So he built a separate house for her across the Kidron on a place called to this day "The Mount of Offence" because of this very fact.

There may have been political reasoning behind this marriage, since there certainly seemed to be strategical gain in the fact that Pharaoh's daughter brought as part of her dowry the fortress city of Gezer already referred to as having been "taken" by Pharaoh in the first place. This Gezer became important in the whole defence bastion of the south and west. The move may also have assured the friendship of the greatest power to the west. It was, however, a flagrant violation of a clear command from God: "You shall not intermarry with them, nor they with you, for surely they will turn away your hearts after their gods." (11:2). This is exactly what happened, as later Scriptures abundantly show.

Throughout their generations Israel was also to remember that Egypt represented everything from which they had been redeemed at the Exodus and they were never to go down there or have any relations with that nation in any way forever. This was one of the reasons for the yearly Passover supper: it was a calling to remembrance all the experience in Egypt. To imagine that we can further God's work by any sort of expediency, compromise, or disobedience was then, and is now, folly rather than wisdom.

Yet in spite of this Solomon gave a wonderful sermon at the dedication of the Temple, and prayed a wonderful prayer, one of the longest on record. Both were quite right and true and were so recognised by God in His grace even though shortly thereafter, as we have above noticed, God warned Solomon of the danger of any kind of disobedience of His word.

Solomon's son Rehoboam, who succeeded him, was born of an Ammonite princess (1 Kings 14:21). Indeed it is a strange fact that there seems to be no record in Scripture of any other son of Solomon, and stranger still there seems no record of any Israelitish wife taken by Solomon. One wonders if the "young men" consulted with such dire results by Rehoboam were not new palace favourites from Ammon. We must also remember that by his disobedience Solomon brought loss and trouble to Rehoboam's generation and many generations after his time.

It is always wise to look beyond immediate results to indirect but nonetheless serious consequences further ahead. The Egyptian wife was only a beginning, for Solomon went ahead and had wives from Moab, Ammon, Edom, Sidon and the Hittites (11:1). They turned his heart away from God for he built altars and in some cases temples for the gods of these nations, including even Molech, the god who was served with human sacrifices. It is very sad that the man who built the beautiful house of the Lord should later on have built other temples for gods hated by Jehovah. Indeed it is always sad when what was once built for God is destroyed thoughtlessly. Yet it is highly probable that much of this would have been approved and even applauded by the worldly-wise of his day. To have things on a bigger and grander scale would attract attention, draw outsiders, and appeal to all who deal in numbers, bulk and activity. This king had more and bigger of everything: soldiers, chariots, horses, wealth, wives and broadminded links with the nations around, though God had prohibited all of this. He had also developed a philosophy regarding the Hittites, Ammonites, Perizzites, Hivites, and Jebusites. Instead of dealing with them as God has commanded he decided to use them as slaves and taxpayers. These were later to cause great trouble to his successors.

We need go no further; we have shown clearly enough the causes of Israel's declension which should help us understand the pathway to restoration taken by Hezekiah, Josiah and Ezra. Departure from the Word or violation of its teachings brought spiritual ruin. Return to the Word was the only cure, without which no rearranging of programmes, no modernising of temple worship, no restructuring of priesthood, sacrifices, or feasts could help. Indeed such plans would only bring further departure.

Chapter 7

Revival under Hezekiah: Preparation by God

1. Hezekiah's Times

THERE were serious attempts under Asa, Judah's third king, and Jehoshaphat his son to get back to God. These started well but ended in failure, each for a different reason, but we shall examine these later in a separate study. It is as important to note why some attempts failed as to learn why others succeeded.

The revival under godly king Hezekiah was long in coming and the nation had gradually sunk from the heights it once occupied into division, endless wars most of which left Israel in worse condition than before, and the crowning sin of idolatry. God had told Solomon that because of his sin the nation would be torn in two, and this duly happened under the reign of his son Rehoboam. The man who led the revolt of the ten northern tribes was Jeroboam, and after the successful revolt this man became king over what became known as Israel, while Judah and Levi remained loyal to the house of David under the name of Judah. An interesting twist in this story is that when Solomon tried to execute Jeroboam for his sedition the latter fled to Egypt where he was welcomed by king Shishak who later used him as a pawn in his intrigues against Israel. So much for Solomon's fatal alliance with the Pharaoh at an earlier date and sealed by marriage to Egypt's princess!

Eleven kings had followed Solomon over Judah before the succession of Hezekiah and, as we have mentioned, two of them had started revivals which were flawed and failed to bear fruit. Before studying the revival which took place under this man we must look briefly at his background, and the conditions which made revival so necessary.

Hezekiah was born in tumultuous times, and if ever a man had warning of the results of departure from God it was he. His great-grandfather Uzziah, also called Azariah, who did so well in many ways, was removed from the throne stricken with leprosy to die in seclusion, because he rashly overrode the Biblical law allowing only the family of Aaron to function as priests. This Uzziah was obviously a capable man, achieving success in building, fortifying, reorganising and directing armies and extending Israel's frontiers, yet there was a weak link in the chain: "When he was strong, his heart was lifted up to his destruction, for he transgressed against the Lord his God by entering the temple of the Lord to burn incense" (2 Chron 26:16). Pride and arrogance destroy all hope of revival.

Hezekiah's grandfather, Jotham, appears to have been a good man at heart, upright in personal life, as well as being a brave and successful ruler in many ways. He fought and conquered some surrounding enemies, built cities in regained territory and rebuilt or repaired defensive walls, but he never attempted anything like spiritual revival in the nation for "still the people acted corruptly" (2 Chron 27:1-9). Also the "high places (centres of idol worship or of a corrupted worship of God) were not removed; the people still offered sacrifices and burned incense on the high places" (2 Kings 15:32-35). In other words, he appears as a good man, but in God's things ineffective, lacking spiritual vision or authority.

Hezekiah's father, Ahaz, his immediate predecessor on Israel's throne, "walked in the ways of the kings of Israel (the northern kingdom now sunk in idolatry), indeed he made his son pass through the fire according to the abomination of the nations (human sacrifice to Molech), and sacrificed and burned incense on the high places and under every green tree" (2 Kings 16:1-4). We mentioned earlier long range consequences of departure from the word of God, and here is a clear example of this. Molech was the fire-god called by the Lord "the abomination of Ammon". How sad it is to think that Solomon built a high place to Molech in the hill before Jerusalem, probably for the Ammonite queen he had married, the mother of Rehoboam.

Ahaz was attacked by the united forces of Israel and Syria and, since he had lost the delivering power of the Lord through his disobedience, he looted the treasuries of the house of God to buy help from the king of Assyria. The wily Assyrian monarch accepted all the money but "came and distressed him and did not assist him" (2 Chron 28:20). On top of this came the Edomites and Philistines killing, plundering, taking captives and occupying large areas of Judah and "dwelling there . . . for the Lord brought Judah low because of Ahaz" (v. 19). Defeated by Syria he sacrificed to the gods of Damascus which had defeated him saying: "Because the gods of the kings of Syria help them, I will sacrifice to them that they may help me". But they were the ruin of the whole nation. We need not follow the details of the complete slide into idolatry and disaster which came from this course. The lesson for us is clear: trying to gain success by copying the religious patterns of the world around us brings ruin, not revival or renewal. Thus Hezekiah's father, grandfather and great-grandfather should have been warnings.

2. The Assyrian Invasion and Israel's Deportation

Hezekiah had an even more impressive lesson on the results of departure from the word of God, one which would have struck terror to any heart. He came to the throne of Judah when the break-away northern kingdom of Israel was in the final throes of disintegration because of its sin. This northern kingdom had had nineteen kings of four different dynasties, quite a few of them assassinated. There never was a hint of revival or of turning to God from the prevailing idolatry which had been established by their first king, Jeroboam, who set up the golden bulls of Egypt at Dan and Bethel. God had sent prophets to them but they either ignored or effectively silenced them, until nothing remained but judgment.

When Hezekiah began his reign in Jerusalem there remained but six years until Shalmaneser, head of the fast-rising Assyrian empire, invaded and defeated this northern kingdom, deporting masses of the people (2 Kings 18:11). The totally decadent nation of the north had its last five kings in a period of less than 33 years, one for two years, one for six months, one for one month, and several of these were murdered. The lesson could not have been more awesome, or presented in clearer terms. As far back as Lev 26:27-33 God had warned: "If you do not obey me . . . I will bring desolation, and your enemies who dwell in it (the land) shall be astonished at it. I will scatter you among the nations" etc. This had now happened to the northern kingdom, the borders of which lay a mere twenty miles from Jerusalem and much less from other cities. It was here on that border that Jeroboam had placed his golden bull, in defiance of God and to coax people away from the temple in Jerusalem and its worship.

The horrifying details of the Assyrian campaign must have been common knowledge in Judah: the slaughter of armies, the plundering and destroying of cities along with much of the population, and the uprooting of those remaining to a strange land beyond the Euphrates. Hezekiah would have seen all this and must have been deeply impressed. The lesson was clear: rebellion's price is high.

3. Warning Signs in Judah

When Hezekiah came to the throne the results of his father's sixteen year reign were also everywhere to be seen: the altars of Molech where his son, Hezekiah's brother, had

been made to "pass through the fire", the Baals, the
Asherah, the high places, the groves, in fact all the very
things that would bring judgment on the northern
kingdom. Worse still the temple had been robbed and
stripped, its treasures stolen to try to buy off these very
pagan nations involved in the north, exactly as that
northern kingdom had tried to buy off its enemies. Finally
the temple itself was now shut up to hide the fact that its
gold and silver furniture and decorations, all pictures and
types of the coming Messiah Himself according to the
Hebrews letter, had been taken to build altars to other gods.
If, in spite of all this, there was any doubt in Hezekiah's
mind as to his nation's fate should the people not turn back
to God in repentance, three of the great prophets were at
the height of their ministry, Isaiah, Hosea, Micah and
perhaps Nahum, and we have their writings with warnings
clear and unambiguous. They had begged for a return to
God.

4. Godly influences upon Hezekiah

We speak of "Hezekiah's" revival merely for convenience
since the prophets just mentioned must be given a great
share of the credit. This is just to remind us that the most
prominent names are not always of the people exerting the
strongest spiritual influence. "In the year that king Uzziah
died" Isaiah had had his great vision of the majesty, power,
and holiness of God whose throne was above every other
throne (Isa 6). We know that Uzziah's son, Jotham, "was
over the king's house (as regent) judging the people of the
land" (2 Chron 26: 21) for an unspecified period while his
father lived on, a living monument to God's judgment on
disobedience, even with good intentions in holy things.
Isaiah had lived through all this in the reigns of Uzziah,
Jotham and Ahaz, and now into that of Hezekiah, so he
must have been a very old man with much experience of
God and His ways. His close relations with Hezekiah are
evident from Isa 37, 2 Kings 19 and 2 Chron 32:20 where

they pray together in the temple about the invasion of the land by Sennacherib, the new king of Assyria.

There are other interesting links for we read that Hezekiah's mother was daughter of Zechariah, thought by some to be a descendent of one murdered by Jehoash, and in 2 Chron 26:5 we read that Uzziah (the grandfather) had "sought God in the days of Zechariah, who had understanding in the visions of God". Some texts have "fear" instead of "visions" which is also significant. How interesting it will be one day to have the whole story of all these less visible links. That this would have something to do with the fact that "in the first year of his reign, and the first month" and even according to 2 Chron 29:17 on the first day, "Hezekiah opened the doors of the house of the Lord and repaired them." He had been taught long before he came to the throne. There was a godly remnant under the surface.

5. The Standard and Pattern of David

Attention must again be called to the words: "He did what was right in the eyes of the Lord, according to all that his father David had done" (2 Chron 29:2). Some in our day would call this at best traditionalism, at worst lack of independent thinking, or even being in a rut. We constantly hear the cry for original thinking, breaking with our past, spreading our sails to new winds, experimenting with new ideas. If Timothy were alive to-day he might be told that Paul's idea of "being an imitator of (him)" would be old-fashioned and restrict growth. We hardly dare to think of the derision he would face for continuing in "the faith of his mother and even of his grandmother", even though it was their instruction in his childhood which had brought him under the authority of the "sacred writings". We may well see the day when *"Faith of our fathers"* will be removed from our hymnbooks to make room for something more progressive. David's lifelong devotion to God's word and God's house was, as we have already noted, a standard by which all succeeding kings would be judged and evaluated.

Chapter 8

Revival under Hezekiah: Its Execution

1. Hezekiah's First Steps

THUS prepared even before his coronation, no time was lost in waiting until his reign was established politically, his army trained, and his cabinet in place. He would not take polls to find out percentages of those open to change, or do inductive studies to find out if he had a majority with him, or search for a consensus, much less call in specialists from the surrounding nations to benefit from their expertise in such matters. For him, all the instructions regarding God's house were found in God's word and he also knew that they were found nowhere else. He had God's word, and faithful, experienced men of God around him who could expound that Word. The Word contained all the information about the plans of David and Solomon for the building of the Temple, and the full report of its consecration and filling by the Spirit and glory of God. This would include all the teaching for the duties and privileges of priests and Levites, offerings and sacrifices, as well as yearly feasts of Jehovah etc. He did not need the help of worldlings who knew nothing about God or revival. He saw the abandoned, plundered, and desecrated house of God. He also saw the idol temples and altars built in many cases with materials taken from the temple, while pillars, high places, and groves were everywhere. He and his people only needed to follow those instructions in obedient dependence on God and to start without delay or questioning. Of course there was repentance, sorrow for sin, recognition of departure, as seen for example in 2 Chron 29:6-9; 30:22. Note the mention of sin and trespass offerings.

It is worth noticing that Hezekiah began with the house itself, and not with the idols outside. The house of the Lord

51

was in sad condition, with doors closed and desolation inside, with all sorts of "filth" to be dealt with. God's house was, above and before all else, HIS dwelling, and the king recognised that they owed it to God that it should be in a fit condition for His occupation. This house was very precious to the king because it was precious to God, the place where He chose to put His name. Yet much that was precious had been losts from it, traded away in exchange for convenience and the satisfaction of their enemies. It was also cluttered with the dirt and rubble of many unholy invasions of its sacredness. All of this must be dealt with as a beginning in any thought of restoration or revival. If God's house, His dwelling which is also His witness, is unclean there can be no blessing and this is where revival must start.

We must confess with sorrow that in many respects this is a picture of not a few assemblies or local churches today. Perhaps we need to remind ourselves that the church universal and also the local church are referred to as the temple and dwelling of God. A reading of 1 Cor 3:16-17; 2 Cor 6:16; Eph 2:21-22; 1 Tim 3:15; Heb 3:6; and 1 Pet 2:5 would, we believe, put this beyond doubt. Yet in all the writing and talking of our days, how often do we hear anything about maintaining the holiness and purity of God's house as one of the first steps toward revival? Indeed we rarely even hear mention of the concept of the local assembly as God's house or temple at all.

Revival would demand a serious house cleaning, a carefulness to maintain the sanctity of it, especially when we are reminded in 1 Cor 3 that whoever defiles that temple will himself be defiled, or marred, by God. In the same context in 1 Cor 5 it is required that sin in the local church must be dealt with and put away as a destructive leaven that, if left, will permeate the whole congregation. But the leaven of malice and wickedness, as well as the "old leaven" or the leaven of the things of the past life must also be dealt with. In all the talk of reorganising, restructuring and educated ministry, we seem to have lost sight of the holiness of the local church and the need for maintaining it. Purity of life, purity of practice and purity of doctrine surely become the house of God, yet this purity is sadly neglected in most of the suggestions for revival this writer has come across.

The house must also be opened and repaired. That is, it must be opened to make it accessible to the people of God. It must also be repaired so that it would be functional and operable by them. In the days of Ahaz the house was shut up because it had become unimportant: other methods and places of worship were considered more important, more convenient, or more attractive to people. Later, in Josiah's day, he complained that the people had turned their faces from the temple, and the same was true here. They could live without it, whereas God had intended it to be central to every individual and every life. This had been so from the days of the tabernacle. That dwelling of God was erected first, and was in the centre; every home took its proper place around it.

We cannot help seeing another failure in our own day when, far from being the centre of our lives, in many cases the assembly is for Sunday and maybe just for the one meeting on that day which *we* consider most to our liking. If the assembly is God's temple and dwelling for this age, indeed the only thing He has or takes delight in during the age, then it certainly should be the centre of our thinking, planning and living, something which we hold precious and to which we have a deep and sincere commitment. It is not merely a mission hall where the Gospel is preached and people brought to Christ (though it certainly should be a centre of Gospel activity). It is, before all else, God's dwelling and, as such, God's witness to the world, the expression of His character. We also too easily fall into the habit of calling it "our" assembly or church. It might give us a better perspective if we made ourselves think of it as

"God's" church or assembly, as the NT calls it. It is attacked by the world, the flesh and the devil. There is constant failure and breaking down which, as in Hezekiah's day, calls for constant spiritual repair. This should be a deep concern of every Christian, but very particularly of the overseers or elders, instead of merely judging the health of the assembly by a head count or preening ourselves on our activities or the number of young people we have, without much concern for the quality of spiritual life evidenced by young and old. Ps 93 sums it up well when it says: "Holiness becometh thy house". "Worship the Lord in the beauty of holiness" (1 Chron 16:29).

2. Sanctification of Priests and Levites

But as well as a cleaned and repaired house there must be a people in proper spiritual condition to serve and worship in it. In 2 Chron 29 before the king approached the people as a whole he dealt with those responsible for service in the house of God. The priests were those more particularly connected with the offerings and sacrifices, symbolic of worship. The Levites dealt with the more mechanical functions around the temple. In the days of the tabernacle, the Levites assembled and erected it, saw to its transportation; in the case of the ark they carried it, and in general dealt with the upkeep of the whole structure. They were also responsible for guarding and protecting it, and many other services; in short they were the servants of the Lord's house. We badly need more servants to-day, devoted souls working for God in His house. But the Levites were also teachers (Deut 24:8; 33:8-10; with 2 Chron 17:8-9; 35: 3-4), and we certainly need teachers, perhaps more than anything.

a. Worship, Then and Now

While Levites and Levitical service were very important as forming a large and valuable part of the work of the tabernacle and later of temple as considered above, priests and priesthood were also very important in the king's mind. Priests and priesthood were the living link between God and His people. But they had to be called, and could only fulfil their duty when sanctified and purified. A cleansed house and a called priesthood would have neither value nor meaning if the priests were not in a proper condition to stand in God's presence. They must be sanctified, or set apart for God, and they must be clean. If, as we believe, worship is a basic indication of spiritual condition then in our day we are in serious trouble. In OT days a representative priesthood vested in the family of Aaron maintained a constant flow of worship to God from His people, but the NT teaches us that every believer is a priest who should be able to carry out his service of worship intelligently. It would seem to-day that worship is little understood and also that there is much confusion as to its practice. We now hear people welcomed "to worship with us this morning" when a good number of those addressed are not Christians at all and the meeting is convened that they might hear the Gospel. To many, the Lord's supper, where we gather to remember Him and proclaim His death, is little more than a thanksgiving and praise service. In many cases there is little more than thanking God for what He has done for *us* and what *we* have received, whereas worship is basically a giving to God rather than a receiving from Him. Some would even want it changed into a "sharing meeting". There may be time and place for such sharing providing it is mutually profitable and not a return to Oxford Group Buchmanism, but this is far removed from what worship is.

b. Worship: What Is It?

In Scripture worship is seen as bringing to God something which speaks of His Son, something for His satisfaction and something on which He can feast and in which He can delight. The priests of the OT entered God's presence either with blood, speaking of the value of the death of Christ, or with parts of the offerings filling their hands lifted up to God, speaking of different aspects of the person of Christ, or with incense speaking of the holy aroma of His perfect life.

In Deut 26:1-11 we have an illustration of worship. It anticipated Israel's coming into the land, the place of full blessing which God had always meant them to possess and enjoy, and a foreshadowing of our spiritual place of blessing in Christ in the heavenlies. They were to possess it and dwell in it as well as cultivate it. They were to lay hold of what God had for them and to live in the good of it. They were then to take of the fruit of that land, put it in a basket, and bring it to the priest. Laying it down before the Lord, they would "worship before the Lord [their] God". Before there could be worship there had to be entrance into the land, possession of it, cultivation of it and the filling of the basket. Surely the fruit in the basket came from seed put in the ground to die and spring up in abundant reproduction; to us it is a figure of our blessed Lord, the "corn of wheat which fell into the ground and died". We see Christ in resurrection and in all His abundant fruitfulness. The worshipper came with his basket full of that which spoke of Christ, for the satisfaction of God.

It is also important to notice that in connection with the feasts of Jehovah all the males were to appear before the Lord at least three times each year for the three groups of feasts, and that no male was to appear before God empty (Deut 16:16). If all were to come with this on their hearts to-day we would have vastly different worship and remembrance meetings. Of course it takes time, feeding on the Scriptures and meditation to prepare for such worship, and maybe this is the reason for such sterility and boredom in what should be the very highest point of holy joy and deepest yearning of the Christian heart. Alas life in our society leaves little time or quiet for such preparation unless we are prepared to pay the price and budget our time, rearranging our lives to have something for God instead of dashing out to such a meeting with our minds full of other things that help little in worship.

If every heart was full of Christ and every spirit under the power and influence of the Holy Spirit there would be no need for arranged speakers at the remembrance meeting and even less for a chairman who decides what the theme should be and who would "exercise a certain amount of control over the meeting" as has been suggested. The misunderstanding here is in confusing ministry with worship. It would also, perhaps, make us less dependent on our hymnbooks to fill in the gaps. We would also be saved from the blunder of evaluating the worship meeting in terms of what we may or may not get out of it. Worship should be thought of in terms of what God gets out of it.

One other thought should clinch for us this whole matter of worship. In Lev 21:6, 17, 21, 22 we are told that the offerings presented to God on the great brazen altar of the tabernacle, and later the temple, were the "bread" or "food" of God. We find the same usage, among other places, in Lev 3:11 and Num 28:2, while in Mal 1:7, 12 the same altar is called "the table of the Lord" or "my table". In Ezek 41:22 the same is said of the altar of incense, where this was burned constantly as a symbol of the perfume of the perfections of Christ in life and in death before the Father. Ezek 44:16 refers to the brazen altar in the same way and to the priests as ministering to [God] at His table. The priests brought to God that which spoke of the glories, perfections and sacrifice of the Son who was yet to come. They were a perfect picture of the believer worshipping by bringing before God in adoration his appreciation of Christ so that the Father's heart may be satisfied in what is brought. We feed on the Word in ministry meetings; in worship God feeds on the spiritual sacrifices we bring to Him (1 Pet 2:5).

How wise was Hezekiah in beginning with the restoration of true prestly and Levitical service in sanctification and

holiness within the house of God, before attempting to deal
with outward ceremony, feasts, offerings or even with the
removal of idols. God's place of majesty and centrality must
be re-established, His house opened and used, His priests
serving Him in sacrifices and incense (2 Chron 29:11). All this
has lessons for us if we are to have true revival. God must
have His place of supremacy and centrality in worship. To
some this may seem far removed from revival, but we are
convinced that in any true revival God's place as the object
of the worship of His people must have priority.

3. Temple Worship Re-established

With the cleansing of God's house completed, with the
accumulated rubbish of the reign of Ahaz thrown into the
Kidron valley, with the furnishings of the house all in their
proper place, the next great step could be taken. The "set
feasts of Jehovah" would be recognised as appointed by
Him. The sacrifices would be offered as the very essence of
their worship.

Where for many years there had been nothing for God,
He was now the centre of everyone's thoughts and
adoration. For generations they had sought for ways out of
their sad condition of spiritual disaster, but always in the
wrong direction. They had followed the pagan concepts of
the surrounding societies, thinking that each one promised
some sort of deliverance. But they sank deeper all the time
into a morass of defeat, and bondage to the very things and
people from whom they sought the deliverance.

The God who had redeemed them from one of these
nations by blood and power in the first place had said:
"Israel is my son, even my firstborn . . . let my son go that
he may serve me" (Exod 4:22-23). In the same book the
meaning of this is made even clearer by the words: "Let my
people go that they may hold a feast unto me." In 10:25
when Pharaoh offered to let them go if their cattle
remained behind, Moses refused since they must have cattle
to offer to God as sacrifices and burnt offerings. Offerings

were basic to the whole purpose of their redemption, as is confirmed and explained in detail by what took place at Mount Sinai, related in Exodus, Leviticus, and Numbers.

They had fallen far from all of this by the end of the reign of Ahaz, and Hezekiah knew better than to imagine that any merely cosmetic changes would satisfy God or bring about the spiritual revitalisation of His people. The first thing to be recognised was that God's place had been taken by other things. They had been giving to other gods what should have been given to the Lord. The altars were cold, the songs had died out, the priesthood was perverted and ignored, basically because God was no longer in His proper place in their hearts, and the people had lost any idea of what true worship was. Now all is different, their hearts are willing and free (29:31), and engaged in the business of bringing to God that which will satisfy His heart because it speaks to Him of the Son whom, one day, He will reveal for the accomplishment of all His purposes and plans.

In 29:20 it is instructive to note that Hezekiah began with the rulers, the mature and respected leaders of the nation. It is here that the work of revival started — with the priests, Levites, leaders — and from there it swept out to the mass of the people.

4. The Offerings Brought

First we must note that their concern in 2 Chron 29:21 was to bring something to God. He must get from His people that for which His heart longed. They were not thinking of expansion, nor of looking better in the eyes of their contemporaries. God Himself, and His desires as expressed in His word, were filling every heart. He was now given first place and to please Him was clearly their one desire. In NT words they were seeking first the sovereignty of God and His righteousness, knowing that when this was fulfilled all else would fall into its proper place. We err when we neglect or ignore this divine principle.

Sin offerings were first brought, for no other offerings would be acceptable if sin was not put away. These offerings were not for their salvation, for they were a people saved by blood in Egypt and brought out by redeeming power. At Mount Sinai they had been brought into covenant relationship with God, again by blood. They were, however, conscious that as His people they had sinned and that this must be confessed and cleansed.

Seven of each class of animal were now brought for a sin offering. Seven in Scripture indicates what is complete or perfect, divine perfection. Evidently the completeness or depth of the consciousness of their sin is emphasises. These offerings were offered "for the kingdom, for the sanctuary, and for Judah" (2 Chron 29:21). The kingdom refers to the nation as related to God and His authority, the sanctuary to His dwelling and testimony which had been violated, and Judah to the people themselves as individuals.

The king and the people laid their hands on the heads of the animals while atonement was made, thus showing complete identification with the sacrifice and acceptance of its fulness to deal with their sin. Then, and only then, were the burnt offerings of true worship brought forward (29:24). Sin must be dealt with before worship can be accepted, yet this is a theme little mentioned in many of the prescriptions for renewal in our day. Theological training, philosophies of ministry, and brightening of services get a lot more emphasis than does our sin and departure from the Scriptures and the need for confession of our lack of devotion to the Lord.

When God received this worship of the burnt offering there was a great spontaneous outburst of praise and song. It was not something invented or revised to meet the desires or tastes of a new generation, but "according to the commandment of David, and of Gad the seer, and Nathan the prophet (v. 25). The instruments used were those of David and the trumpets those of silver, made from the redemption coins.

The other trumpet, the "shophar", was used for warnings, alarms and the marking of the solemn feasts etc. These silver trumpets were used for the Jubilee and other times of special joy and celebration. The joyous outburst of v. 27 is worth quoting in full: "Hezekiah commanded to offer the burnt offering on the altar. And when the burnt offering began, the song of the Lord began also with the trumpets and with the instruments ordained by David the king of Israel. And all the congregation worshipped and the singers sang, and the trumpeters sounded, and all this continued until the burnt offering was finished". It was the sense of giving to God the worship which His heart desired that stirred such spontaneous singing: such singing is not something included in the service for the satisfaction or entertainment of those present. Indeed singing in Scripture is, in general, directed to God in praise, thanksgiving and worship.

Following this worship and praise we find "sacrifices and thank-offerings" pouring in, and we learn from other Scripture references that these were designated in large part for the support of the priests and Levites as well as for the general upkeep of the house of the Lord (vv. 31-33). When the heart is right with God and He is receiving proper worship there will be little need for urging the saints to give, or for engaging in begging to the dishonour of His name. Liberality will always characterise those whose hearts are going out to Him in affection, since all that is given to God's work is given first to Him.

Drink offerings followed, which symbolised the joy of giving, and peace offerings, symbolising fellowship and communion (Lev 7:11ff); portions of them were eaten by both offerer and officiating priest. When God is given His proper place and portion there is always a renewing and

strengthening of fellowship and communion; there is a
sense of being associated with God in what concerns His
house, and a linking with those who form part of it in both
privilege and responsibility.

There is a felt need for more of this spirit and attitude in
"God's house" to-day. Read carefully 1 Pet 2:5; Eph 2:13;
1 Tim 3:12; Gal 6:10. This stage of the revival closes with the
words: "Hezekiah rejoiced, and all the people, that God had
prepared the people" (v. 36). God was given all the glory for
the whole movement; nothing was attributed to their own ·
ability, strength, or planning. Even a little of this spirit of
humility and dependence on God would become us in our
present situation.

Chapter 9

Revival under Hezekiah: Its Results

1. Restoration of Unity

THE return to God with all the consequent rejoicing together in national oneness was a new experience. This bringing together of God's people in the power of the Holy Spirit touched their now-sensitive hearts with thoughts of the divided condition of the ten tribes of the north from the two of the south. Spiritual revival brought about a seeking for unity, not a union hammered out in prolonged bargaining around a table, but a yearning for oneness enjoyed around the altar. True revival joy will never leave behind it a trail of division, alienation, and grief.

Such revival joy stirred Hezekiah to appeal to the estranged tribes of the northern kingdom to come and join them. It would appear that the Assyrian invasion with its destruction and deportations had occurred before this time and the chastened remnant remaining in the land were more open to such advances. Messengers were sent to "All Israel and Judah", and several tribes were singled out for special appeal: "Ephraim, Manasseh, Zebulun, Asher, and Issachar". From Beer-Sheba to Dan the call went out (2 Chron 30:5) and while some refused and mocked, many came. It should be noted that this expression of oneness and great joy was not based on perceptions of their righteousness, much less on a desire to have a bigger company at Jerusalem as proof of the success of the new movement. The words are clear: "Keep the passover unto Jehovah Elohim of Israel, for they had not done it for a long time as it had been written" (30:5). What moved them was obviously a desire for obedience to the written Word without consideration of the results in numbers or appearance.

An expansion of the above summary is given in vv. 6-9 of the same chapter in which some very key expressions stand out: "Turn again unto the God of Abraham, Isaac, and Israel . . . yield yourselves unto the Lord God and enter into His sanctuary . . . and serve Him (that is in worship)". The results are detailed in v. 11: "(they) humbled themselves and came to Jerusalem ... with one heart to do the commandment of the king by the word of the Lord". Oneness of heart in turning to God in repentance will break down many a carnal barrier and will bring about a unity of spirit as we make our way together in tears into the sanctuary.

2. Further Results of Revival

Having tasted the joys of obeying the word of God and experiencing the delights and holiness of the sanctuary, a number of other results followed quickly. The feasts of passover and unleavened bread were reinstated and kept by "a very great number". Passover was their remembrance feast because of that great night on which they were saved from the destroyer, and then for ever delivered by power from the bondage of Egypt and all its ways. From the latter part of this chapter, and also from Josiah's revival we gather that Israel had not been as careful to observe this feast as they should. Now they were getting back to basics, and found such delight in this that they asked permission to keep it for a further seven days, something we do not read of ever again in the Bible, giving us a glimpse of the ecstasy which accompanies the recovery of lost truth and obedience to it.

Passover spoke to them of redemption, deliverance, the end of an old life of bondage and futility. Unleavened bread spoke of the character of the new life into which passover introduced them. These two feasts were the very foundation of all other feasts and indeed of all sacrifices and functions of the tabernacle, the temple, and all Israelitish life. They had been instituted in Egypt long before any of the others were given, even a priesthood or instructions about approaching God. All of these last are found toward the end of Israel's stay at Sinai and therefore about a year after the Exodus.

a. Lessons from the Passover

We too have a remembrance feast, instituted by the Lord Jesus Himself on the night of His betrayal. We are commanded to keep it: 1 Cor 11 says that we keep it "until he come". Nothing could be more simple or moving than the circumstances and surroundings of that last night when in some private home, the passover supper having ended, the Lord took ordinary bread from the table, broke it, and passed it around to the disciples with the instruction, "Do this, as often as ye eat it, in remembrance of me". The loaf is said, in the Corinthian passage cited above, to be a symbol of His body, as the cup was stated by Himself to be "the new covenant in [His] blood". Scripture does not tell us the day of the week on which our Lord died but it does tell us, repeatedly and specifically, the day of His resurrection, which the earliest Christians called "the Lord's day" and it apparently was on this day that they kept "the Lord's Supper" (see Acts 20:7).

i. The Corruption of the Lord's Supper

Shortly after apostolic days, this very simple feast, surrounded by no ritual, rules, or ceremony, was gradually corrupted until it became a "means of grace", something which gave some sort of mystical help to the Christian, then a means of salvation, the finally "the holy eucharist" and even the "sacrifice of the mass." In such conditions it could only be presided over by a clergyman who must be ordained by a bishop or equivalent, who in turn must be consecrated by an archbishop and so on up the chain of ecclesiastical authority, invented in its entirety by men, and for which there is not a word of support in Holy Scripture.

In this way almost the whole meaning of the simple

remembrance supper was lost, except to that remnant who through the ages clung tenaciously to it as the very symbol and centre of fellowship and communion. Nearly 170 years ago others, many of them in the very clerical system we have referred to, through the study of the Scriptures and guided by the Holy Spirit, rediscovered the importance and the beauty of this simple remembrance feast and made it the centre of their fellowship as believers. As in Hezekiah's day, obedience to truth brought fresh discoveries of truth and great joy as each step was taken in practising what they had found. Alas! much of this seems again to be in the process of corruption through lack of understanding of its true character.

From a simple remembrance of Him this remembrance supper has gradually changed, even among those who once knew better, into a "service of worship" with the time allocated ever shortening. Some have timetabled a particular point in that service when the bread and cup should be passed around, neither sooner nor later. A certain format is to be followed with a certain number of hymns sung, often more hymns than anything else, though there is no indication whatever that hymns or even Psalms were used during the first supper. They simply "sang a hymn and went out". We are finding that in an increasing number of such gatherings someone is "put in charge" of opening and even giving of ministry on a regular basis, which makes it easier for those who have no burden or exercise about the direction of the Holy Spirit who represents the Lord there. Some suggest a set programme of Scripture reading to be followed over a specified period; some want a projector present for the learning of more inspirational choruses with modern tunes; some, forgetting the emphasis on the remembrance of the Lord, suggest that it should be turned into a "sharing meeting" where we could exchange information about our experiences. We have even heard of an assembly where sisters engaged in "interpretive dancing". Others have suggested that we might have an occasional breaking of bread at the Family Hour just to show what it is and how we do it! When it has been pointed out that this last could lead to confusion and embarrassment in a mixed audience where unconverted people might in ignorance partake of the emblems, the answer has been: "we would not be uncomfortable with that, even if they did". They apparently had forgotten the passage which says that "he that eateth and drinketh (at the Lord's Supper) unworthily, eateth and drinketh judgment to himself" (1 Cor 11:29).

Some feel that women should be free to participate audibly in this "service", obviously a church meeting, in spite of the clear and unmistakeable teaching of Scripture that "women keep silence in the churches, for it is not permitted to them to speak" (1 Cor 14:34; see also 1 Tim 2:11-12). In more and more cases instrumental music intrudes, and one wonders how long it will be until we have soloists presenting their "musical packages" to the audience where we should be presenting worship to God. We have come a long way from the simplicity of the original gathering, which should surely have something of a pattern to guide us.

ii. The Symbolism of the Lord's Supper

The Christian's remembrance supper is not merely another meeting. It is the foundation of all the gatherings of the church, the one in which the very communion and fellowship of the church is expressed in partaking of the bread and the cup communally. The visible symbolism shows that being partakers at the Lord's table, we are in fellowship with Him, and also that "we being many are one bread [loaf], one body". A reading of 1 Cor 10, 11 should make this clear. Indeed it must be emphasised that everything connected with the Lord's supper is highly symbolic. The table is a symbol of that mentioned in ch. 10

at which all believers constantly feast with the Lord Himself. Joint participation at it symbolises oneness with Him and all who are His (v. 17). The bread is a symbol of Christ's body, both physical and mystical: "the cup which we bless is it not the communion of the blood of Christ?" (10:16). It must be noted that it is the fact that a number drink from one cup which expresses this communion. In using individual cups this important symbolism is completely lost; indeed the term "individual communion cups" seems to be a contradiction in terms. "Individual" expresses the very opposite of communal. It is said that "the important thing is not the cup but what is in it", but on the contrary, the Scripture never once mentions what is in the cup at the Lord's supper but always refers to the cup. The one time the "fruit of the vine" is mentioned is in the preceding passover. In the Lord's remembrance the cup expresses the very essence of church fellowship and our oneness with the Lord and with all who are truly His (1 Cor 10:16-21). In the next chapter we are, in this remembrance, "proclaiming the Lord's death and until He come". This means that the one whom the world crucified is our Lord. It is noteworthy that in this chapter His title "Lord" occurs seven times in connection with remembrance, indicating that in partaking of it we are declaring our submission to Him as Lord.

All this emphasises the importance of the supper: its symbolism, its solemnity and its sanctity. We believe that any true revival will be accompanied by a re-establishment of the Lord's supper and centrality of the worship associated with it. In many places where "renewal" and progressiveness are stressed, we are surprised to see the Lord's Supper being pushed into the background and relegated to a very secondary level.

b. The Feast of Unleavened Bread

The feasts of passover and unleavened bread were so closely related in God's instructions that the one was never celebrated without the other. Indeed throughout Scripture the names are often interchanged, sometimes passover being used for both, at others unleavened bread also being used for both. In Mark 14:12 we read, "the feast of unleavened bread when the passover is killed". The connection is clear and unmistakeable; all who partook of passover, being covered from the destroyer by the blood of the slain lamb, were ushered into a period where leaven in any form was forbidden and must be searched out and removed. It was not to be found "among you" (that is personally), nor "in your houses" (that is in home and family life), "nor in all your borders" (that is congregationally). This would certainly indicate that leaven spoke to them of what was offensive to God, especially when we further discover that it was strictly and specifically forbidden in all offerings which spoke of the coming Christ. In other words leaven had a richly symbolic meaning.

That leaven was clearly seen as indicative of evil by the learned Hebrew scholar Paul is evident in 1 Cor 5:7-8; in connection with unjudged sin in the local church, he says leaven must be put away before it permeates the whole mass. He also says; "Christ our passover is sacrificed for us, therefore let us keep the feast, not with old leaven, neither with the leaven of malice and wickedness, but with the unleavened bread of sincerity and truth." Two things are clear here.

1. That the Holy Spirit parallels the Lord's supper with the passover.
2. That if Christ is indeed our passover and we are keeping a remembrance feast to Him, then we must now find ourselves in "the days of unleavened bread".

In the passage it would seem that four kinds of leaven are mentioned: the unjudged sin, the old leaven of our old ways and standards, and the leaven of malice and wickedness. All or any of these would seep through the whole company polluting and corrupting it.

Literal leaven or yeast is in itself a fermenting corruption which inflates and puffs up. The flesh in the believer does the same thing. This is why leaven is such an apt picture of this flesh which is offensive to God and has been put by Him in the place of judgment and done away in death with Christ. There is no place in the sacrifice of our worship for "the flesh", in its ethical sense. The feast of unleavened bread lasted seven days. Seven being the number of completeness or totality, the Hebrews (and we too) would grasp that, once delivered from judgment and feeding on the slain lamb they (and we) should be done with all that leaven speaks of, for the rest of their lives.

That leaven speaks of much else besides what is mentioned in the Corinthian passage, is clear from the use of it in other parts of the NT. Our Lord Himself spoke of "the leaven of the *Pharisees*" and interpreted it as hypocrisy. The leaven of the Sadducees, since they are said not to believe in anything spiritual (Acts 23:8 *et al*) would speak of materialism. There is the "leaven of *Herod*"; considering his juggling between the Jews and the Romans in matters political, religious, social and moral, we would have to see this as compromise. Gal 5:9 refers to the leaven of *legalism*.

Matt 13:33 shows a woman introducing leaven into the meal (which, in other places such as the meal offering, speaks of Christ). The leaven in this case we take to be false doctrine, particularly regarding Christ; such false doctrine is prevalent almost everywhere in our day. Leaven was specifically banned in all offerings which spoke of Christ. For the believer who is enjoying his place as redeemed and is feeding on Christ as the passover Lamb there will be a desire, and indeed an obligation, to remove everything of which leaven speaks.

We must also be careful not to restrict this putting away of leaven to its connection with our religious or church life only. As has already been seen it was not to be found in their personal life, their family life, and their broader life in social, business and civic affairs. The term "in all your borders" included every phase throughout the length and breadth of their everyday functioning. It is so easy for us to be careful, even demanding, in our church life on the Lord's day and yet live on a much lower level during the other days of the week. This is, of course, hypocrisy and so leaven of the worst kind, for what we are during the week and in all our interpersonal dealings will affect and colour what we are on the Lord's day.

In all of this we can see how important it was to reinstate all that was symbolised in all of these feasts and offerings, if real revival was to be brought about in Hezekiah's day, and we can be sure that the same applies to our day.

3. The Destruction of Idols

2 Chron 31 informs us that the people, led by the king, went much further than the cleansing and restoration of the temple, the reinstating of the divinely instituted feasts and offerings, and the outpouring of financial giving for the maintenance of everything that pertained to God's house. What followed was the removing and destroying of every kind of idol they could find. If we were to ask ourselves what, in the first place, had led to the terrible conditions which had brought them so low and called down the judgment of God, making revival so necessary, what would be the answer? What was the root cause of the whole backsliding and ruination of their life and testimony? The answer is not hard to find. It was the allowing of other gods to take the place of the one-and-only Jehovah Elohim. Restoration would never be complete until they dealt with this.

In the giving of the commandments, precepts, and ordinances to govern every aspect of their lives – individual, social and religious – the very first word, and that from which all else flowed was: "Thou shalt have no other gods before me". No one and no thing was ever to take the place in their hearts which was rightfully God's. Scriptures, almost without number, promised that if they maintained

God in their hearts' affections, they would be blessed in every way. At the same time they were warned in the most solemn language that if they turned aside and served other gods and worshipped them He would shut up the heaven (there would be no blessing), dry up the earth in barrenness (there would be no fruit) and they would be destroyed (Deut 11:16-17).

The first step of Israel's downward slide, was as we have already noticed in Judges 2:11: "The children of Israel did evil in the sight of the Lord and served the Baalim," and from that point onward this trend became more and more pronounced. A close examination of this development seems to indicate that a lot of this idolatry started from a desire to be like the religions around them. Indeed we have seen that the very first instance of it in the golden calf of Sinai was not a serving of another god so much as worshipping God in an idolatrous way. The second reason seems to have been that they felt that the gods of the other lands helped their worshippers, worked for them and made them successful. This became a trap to Israel.

Are we not in danger of the same folly? Because we see the practices of the religious world around us bringing apparent success in numbers and a growing level of activity, we are tempted to copy their ways and to adopt their goals, almost as gods. Instead of turning back to God and His word in confession of our sin and coldness of heart we think that by copying the methods (using the gods) of the religious world around us, we can be as successful as they. Indeed we are told by some that we should be copying their ways, since they are so successful. This was the beginning of Israel's sin and judgment fell on them because of it. It is high time that we paid attention to these principles of divine dealing.

There were of course other ways in which God's place was usurped. Wealth, comfort, a position of power, recognition in the world, all had a share in their ruination.

We have already dealt with this in the lives of Solomon, Uzziah, and many others who were blessed while they were small but "when they became great they forgot the Lord" (something else was in His place) and they fell. Ours is a society and an age of affluence, pleasure, and comfort where God has no place and where "success" has become a god, whether in the social, business, intellectual, religious or even sports life. We have in many ways become like that world, to our great shame and loss, in spite of so many warnings against loving it or being conformed to it. We worship what is big, and hold up whatever is a success as something to be copied. We find more and more of our Christian articles and books cluttered with the phrases and terminology of that world; its jargon terms litter so many of the articles and books on church growth, church leadership and even "church management" that they give every appearance of having been adapted from the latest books on how to succeed in business or the professions. One sees signs of this at every turn, so that even the names of those writing articles professedly on spiritual things have to have their titles or qualifications prominently displayed. Even qualifications which are as far removed from spiritual things as that the writer is president of a soap manufacturing company get a mention. One wonders what titles like these have to do with ability in Biblical things. Are they simply emblems of an élitism which seems to be so worshipped everywhere? All idols should be dealt with, dethroned, destroyed, whether those of materialism, success, position, power, popularity, or simply vulgar ostentation. If they in any way take the place of God in our vision, they should have, and can have, no place in true spiritual life.

The Holy Spirit sums the whole passage up with the words: "In every work that he (Hezekiah) began in the house of God and in the law and in the commandments, to seek His God, he did it with all his heart and prospered".

It should be clear to any who read these passages with

care that revival is primarily a thing of the heart and spirit. A restored and revived congregation is nothing more than a congregation of spiritually-restored and revived individuals. Instead of blaming others for what we profess to have found wanting in our surveys on them, there will be inner conviction of our own backsliding, sin, lack of heart devotion to Christ, and some genuine repentance and tears for our failure as God's people. This sort of conviction and repentance will surely turn us to more obedience to God's word. It may also make us more humble, and a little less ready to proclaim that anyone wishing to do better in church building should consult us.

Chapter 10

Revival under Hezekiah: Satanic Opposition

Satan's Counter-Attack

WITH all the blessing enjoyed through this turning to God
we are not surprised to read of a vicious attack by the
enemy. Indeed we can be sure that wherever there is a work
of God, even in restoration and revival, it will not go
unchallenged; we should expect testing. God will test the
reality of our spiritual experiences, sifting and
strengthening us in the testing. As in the case of Job and
Hezekiah he may even permit Satan to put us to the proof.

First there came upon Hezekiah's Israel an invasion by
Assyria which, humanly speaking, looked like a total
overthrow. Read 2 Chron 32:1; 2 Kings 18:17; Isa 36, 37.
In face of this threat from which no human power in Judah
could deliver, the king and the prophet Isaiah went to God
and in humility put the whole thing in His hands. The
deliverance was complete, and totally God's doing.

In v. 23 of the Chronicles passage we see the beginning of
another of Satan's wiles. If he could not shake the king by
force and a head-on attack he could use a more crafty tactic.
After the deliverance many people in the surrounding
nations brought to the king gifts, with their congratulations.
What an opportunity for him to give the glory to God and
bear a wonderful testimony to the power of the one true
Jehovah. He may have done this, but, if so, there is no
mention of it, and we do read that Hezekiah "was exalted in
the sight of all nations", and perhaps he enjoyed it. There is
no word of the Lord being exalted which is always what
should happen, especially when in this case the victory was

all God's; neither Hezekiah nor anyone else had a hand in it.

God then tested and humbled the king with a very severe illness and sent a message to him that he would die. He will never exalt the flesh in His child, nor will He give His glory to another. Man in the flesh is put in the place of death. Again there is repentance, an appeal to God, and God graciously restores. Up from the place of death, the whole new life from here on should have been entirely for God and His glory. What a revelation the whole story is of the frailty of man, the pride of man, and his slowness to learn, even when tested more than once in the same way.

Ambassadors come from Babylon, the great new empire on the Euphrates which was taking the place of the waning Assyrian one. What an honour for the king of Judah, and what magnificent presents must have been sent to him by the mighty potentate of the East. God's word had long ago told the king that Israel was to have nothing to do with the surrounding nations, lost as they were in the worst forms of idolatry and demonism. But our very natures respond to flattery in words or deeds and, like the king, we lower our guard.

We learn from 2 Kings 20:12-13 supplemented by 2 Chron 32:27-31, that it is the story of several of the earlier kings ... "He had very great wealth. He made himself treasuries for silver, and for gold, and for precious stones, and for spices, and for shields, and for all manner of costly articles ... moreover he made for himself cities ..." All of this had been prohibited in their king by God Himself, in Deut 17:14-19. The last verse of that chapter tells us that the warning and prohibition was "That his (the king's) heart be not lifted up above his brethren and that he turn not aside from the commandment". As we have seen, Solomon violated this commandment and paid the same price.

From 2 Chron 32:31 we learn that the ambassadors did not come merely to congratulate him on his recovery, and probably his victory over Assyria, but "to inquire of the wonder that was done in the land". The king made the mistake of taking the glory that belonged to God, a mistake to which we are all so prone. His personal pride made him show off everything as though it were his own. Are we not, at least in our measure, guilty of the same thing when we publicise the increasing of our numbers, showing pictures of how much we have enlarged our buildings, highlighting the methods we have used in this, and offering to share our expertise with those less expert? Surely we all need to learn the lesson so clear in what we have studied: that even a great and genuine revival granted by the grace of God can be marred by the intrusion of the flesh and its self-sufficiency.

What an opportunity Hezekiah had to show that all was done by the great Jehovah Elohim who had brought about not only the revival, but also the wonderful visible display of success and his own healing. But Hezekiah acted foolishly, for he also revealed to those who at heart were his enemies, not only the personal but also the national treasury, and on top of that all the "armour . . . treasuries . . . in his house, (and) in all his dominion". This would be the equivalent of one of the Western nations taking their bitterest enemy on a tour of their finance departments, their laboratories, their nuclear plants, the planning centres of their military forces, all their military bases, with complete access to everything. He paid dearly for it because, as God told him plainly, he had opened the gates to the enemy who would finally overwhelm Israel and take away everything he had boasted in. When we try in our arrogance to use the world's ways and tactics, boasting that we can bring about our own success, we can be drawn more deeply into their orbit that we had ever intended, and may awake to our folly when it is too late. It was a tragic ending to a wonderful life. Surely it spells out here for our learning that: "The flesh profiteth nothing" (John 6:63); "We ... have no confidence in the flesh" (Phil 3:3).

Chapter 11

After Hezekiah: Losing Ground

1. Lessons from Revival

THE revival under Hezekiah was a great one and also the first real one in the history of the monarchy. It had far-reaching effects on the northern kingdom as well as in Judah. It had also brought about a measure of restored unity and showed God's hand with them in the matter of the attempted Assyrian invasion. We know, however, that the spirit of revival must be maintained, and the present chapter shows that this did not happen.

The fifty-seven years following Hezekiah's death were disastrous, and therefore call for our attention. During this period Manasseh and Amon reigned, the son and grandson respectively of the godly Hezekiah. The whole sad story is contained in one chapter (2 Chron 33) of a mere twenty-five verses, and there are several lessons we may take from the account.

1. It shows us that ground gained in revival must be guarded constantly and defended with ceaseless vigilance, indeed revival must be a continual and ongoing process. It should never be seen as a spurt or reshuffle which will put us on track and then enable us to sit back. As the coat-of-arms of one of Britain's greatest battleships puts it: "Eternal vigilance is the price of freedom".

2. It shows us also that there is no room for any kind of confidence in the flesh, or in human plans and safeguards.

3. We also learn that while revival and restoration are sweet and real to one generation, the following generations who inherit such blessings without cost, and often

without conviction, are not nearly so impressed with them, and indeed sometimes are ready to give them up without much concern.

2. The Reign of Manasseh

Manasseh came to the throne at twelve years of age and the story of his reign may be put together from 2 Kings 21 and 2 Chron 33. It is a sad but very instructive study, and should be entered upon with a humble heart and a bowed head. If we are honest with ourselves we must know how often the principles involved are true in our own experience. The story shows us that neither revival nor godliness runs in family trees or bloodlines. In the flesh "there is no good thing", and spiritual condition and position must be experienced anew by each individual and generation. There is always that "new generation that knows not the works of the Lord" as we read in Judges; that fatal third generation against whose tendency the political and social philosophers warn us, those who accept a position and even adapt to it for a while without the moral power or determination to maintain it.

The teaching and care of the overseers and parents are very necessary in such cases. It was when the godly teaching of Joshua and those trained by him was no longer available that the declension of the book of Judges set in, and it is ever thus. Each succeeding spiritual generation must be taught the truths enjoyed by the preceding one. The "things received" must be communicated to "faithful men who shall be able to teach others". The instructions given for the annual keeping of the feast of passover "throughout all your generations forever" were given so that when the children asked the meaning of what was being done the parents would have opportunity for instructing that new generation. One might be forgiven for asking if we have been careful in thus instructing our children.

a. The Wickedness of Manasseh

The catalogue of Manasseh's sins covers the whole range

of arrogant evil. "He built again" all that his father had demolished, rearing up altars to Baal, making groves, worshipping the host of heaven (the sun, moon, and star gods with the accompanying astrology imported from Babylon). He built altars for his gods in the house of the Lord, built altars for the host of heaven in both courts of the temple, and caused his son to pass through the fire to Molech. It seems as though some demon was driving him in his frenzied efforts to insult God. Or was he seeking approval from others, or even perhaps to satisfy some of his political overlords in surrounding countries? He dabbled in horoscopes, enchantments, spiritism, and wizards, and crowned it all by putting up in the very house of God "a carved image" which in 2 Kings 21:7 is called an "image of a grove", a gross Asherah or phallic symbol, and with this it would seem that brazen effrontery could go no further.

We are told that he "seduced" the nation into all these evils. Seduction is the power to charm one into something which is not what it appears to be. What the seduction was here we are not told: political expediency, the lure of being like others; the "success in liberation" syndrome; "it works for others, so let's try it". Or there may even have been the tactic of persuading the people that this was the only way to preserve their very existence in view of what was going on around them. Other nations were going ahead in expansion on every side while they were in decline, and the ways of the fathers appeared outdated, disorganised and unproductive. It is an old ploy, but it never fails to work on the minds of the unwary.

Whichever of these reasons may have been in his mind, the passion with which he set out on his course almost forces one to believe that he had lived with a deep resentment in his heart against all his father stood for and felt under some sort of mindless compulsion to smash all his father had built, and rebuild all his father had destroyed.

This sort of reaction has been noted many times in past

history, and sometimes can been observed in our own day and in our own circles. Though the warnings of some of the mightiest and most eloquent of the prophets would still be remembered in his day, he appears to have had no perception of how near he was to the ultimate judgment of God on Judah, bringing with it that nation's destruction and desolation, and also ushering in "the times of the Gentiles" which have continued until the present hour for over 2,600 years. Whatever time Israel would spend in her own land would be under either the protection or the domination of Babylon, Medo-Persia, Greece, Byzantium, Syria, Rome, the Saracens, the Turks, or the British. The Lord spoke to Manasseh and his people, warning them plainly of this, but they would not listen. This poor sin-blinded man in his pride was playing games with God and His word on the very eve of tragedy. "Wherefore the Lord brought upon them the captains of the host of Assyria who took Manasseh with hooks, bound him with bronze fetters, and carried him to Babylon". He became the prisoner of that which he had copied!

b. Manasseh's Repentance

Here in Babylon a strange thing happens. In one of God's mysterious workings of grace this villain who had murdered innocent people until he "filled Jerusalem [with blood] from one end to the other" (2 Kings 21:6), in his affliction humbles himself greatly before the God of his fathers and his prayer is answered. He is returned to Jerusalem, probably as a much-chastened puppet-king, and sets about cleaning up the worst of the idolatrous defilement he himself had introduced there. He casts out the idols, breaks down their altars, removes the strange gods from the house of Lord. He then repairs the altar of the Lord, offers sacrifices thereon, "commanding Judah to serve the Lord God of Israel".

Repentance is a wonderful thing in which we rejoice, but it

is hard, indeed in many cases impossible, to undo completely the results of wrong that has been perpetrated over the course of years. The people continued to sacrifice to the Lord "on the high places". Seeds had been sown which would bear bitter fruit in the future for we read that his son Amon "did that which was evil in the sight of the Lord as did Manasseh his father". It is also rather pathetic to notice in 2 Chron 33:14 that he built a defensive wall around part of the city "to a very great height", and put military captains in all the fortified cities of Judah. This was a classical example of closing the stable door after the horse is stolen. A nice gesture, but much too late. The damage was done; they were already the vassals of Assyria and Babylon.

3. The Reign of Amon

It should be no surprise that Amon would follow the evil his father had done without also following him in his return to God. These are some of the sad results of a bad example. It is so hard to undo, much less to eradicate, the results of sin, even when the sin itself is repented of, confessed, and forgiven, even when restitution and amends have been sincerely attempted.

Abraham could leave Egypt with contrition, a sadder and a wiser man, but he could never undo in his nephew Lot, whom he had taken down with him, the spiritual influence of that disastrous interlude. Quite a while afterwards when in conflict over grazing rights, Lot saw the plain of Sodom "as the garden of the Lord, like the land of Egypt". What a confusion of ideas: Sodom, Eden, and Egypt! He had developed a taste for the irrigated Nile valley and Abraham could now do nothing about that after-effect of his own sin. There was also, of course, the Egyptian slave Hagar and all the further sin and sorrow which she was to cause, although innocently.

David could be forgiven and restored after the affair of Bathsheba, but the results of his sin would not so easily disappear from his own family and household, or even from the heart of Ahithophel, Bathsheba's uncle who turned against David in his hour of great need.

So the sins of Manasseh could be, and were, forgiven, and his zeal in trying to rectify wrongs has to be admired, but there were inevitable results of his wrongdoing which could never be completely eradicated. As soon as Manasseh died and Amon came to the throne, the mass of the people were too ready to lapse into the same old paths, so that after only two years of this man's reign his son Josiah found the nation in a worse state than ever. It is so easy to break down what others have already built at great cost, and so often it can never be rebuilt as before. Weary and saddened hearts have then to live with the results.

Chapter 12

Revival under Josiah: Its Beginnings

1. Early Influences

WE might imagine that after such deliberate and wanton ruination of all that was dear to Him, God would give up the nation. His thoughts, however, are not our thoughts. Perhaps He wished to have it recorded that in the darkest hours before the triple invasion of His sacred land by the Babylonians He could still empower a godly young man as His instrument to bring about perhaps the greatest revival yet. The appearance on the scene of this boy king is so startling and unusual that it must be considered as a special demonstration of the sovereign purpose and power of the Almighty in both the timing and the person involved. Three hundred years earlier an unnamed prophet had foretold the coming of Josiah, even mentioning his name and several specific things that he would do (1 Kings 13). This is obviously in mind in the writing of 2 Kings 23:14-18 when the prophecy was fulfilled.

The results of the revival under Hezekiah, deep and real though they were, had almost entirely disappeared during the next two generations. In that period, as we have seen, Manasseh's personal return to God in his later years appears to have been sincere, yet the damage done proved beyond his power to repair. The very fact of that failure would have been discouraging, as would also the people's speedy lapse into all the worst forms of idolatry.

Hezekiah had been twenty-five years old when he came to the throne and probably had been instructed and trained by the great prophets whose ministry extended throughout his reign. But Josiah was only eight when he began his reign and Jeremiah only began His ministry in the thirteenth year of that reign. We are only told that the brief recorded prophecy of Zephaniah was given "in the days of Josiah" (Zeph 1:1), so Josiah may have had no prophet to influence him during his childhood.

All the failure, all the decay, all the fickleness of the people, all their readiness to fall back so quickly, must have been very daunting to a boy of eight as well as his guides and mentors, whoever they were.

We are almost forced to wonder about his mother of whom so little is said, except that her name was Jedidah, which means "the beloved". Her father's name was Adaiah which means "pleasing to God", though we can only wonder how she was ever married to such a wretch as Amon. May we not see a glimmer here of one who in all the surrounding darkness carried a name to indicate that he was a pleasure to God? All Hebrew names had significance. Was Jedidah one of those people about whom little is said but to whom much is owed? We must also have in mind the names of Hilkiah the priest and Shaphan the scribe who were in charge of the cleansing and repair of the temple and both involved in the finding of the lost Scriptures. And what about the mysterious Huldah to whom a high priest and a scribe had to take the Scriptures for a direct interpretation from the Lord? There are many shadowy figures in the background of all these movements whose roles and activities and influences must await eternity for the full story.

Josiah's youth would also weigh heavily against him in the eyes of many, for age is respected in those lands. Nonetheless this youth was resolved that nothing would push him to the right or left from following "the ways of David his father".

Another telling feature of his reign which might have discouraged him, but did not, was that Judah's days were numbered. It was the end of a dispensation. She appears at this time to have become little better than a vassal state of

Egypt (2 Kings 23:33). Assyria had invaded several times with apparent ease and been bought off by the payment of enormous sums in tribute, except on one occasion when God stepped in because of the prayers of the king and Isaiah, to give totally miraculous deliverance. Now the waning Assyrian empire was giving way to the might of Babylon. (Note that when Manasseh was taken in chains by the Assyrians he was conducted to Babylon.)

In one of Jeremiah's earliest messages God had plainly stated what the end would be and how close it was: "I will bring evil from the north and a great destruction. The lion (with wings this was the emblem of Babylon) is come up from his thicket, and the destroyer of the nations is on his way. He is gone forth from his place to make thy land desolate; and the cities shall be laid without inhabitant . . . He shall come up as clouds, his chariots shall be as a whirlwind: his horses are swifter than eagles. Woe unto us! for we are spoiled. Oh Jerusalem, wash thy heart from wickedness, that thou mayest be saved" (Jer 4:6-14).

It would have been easy for Josiah to say "we are in the last days and things can only get worse, so nothing worthwhile can be done". His job was to do what he could to cleanse the house of God and to "strengthen the things that remain" as was counselled in another last day of departure in Rev 3:2.

2. Dark Days

In historical terms the hour was very late indeed. Josiah would reign 31 years followed by three sons and one grandson who were mere puppets of Egypt and Babylon, and whom F.W. Farrar has called "phantoms of tarnished royalty". The very names of three of them were changed by their masters: Egypt under Pharaoh Necho, and then by the Babylonian Nebuchadnezzar. A sorry pass indeed for David's royal line. So after Josiah a mere twenty and a half years remained before the final curtain in invasion, deportation, and desolation in these three stages as warned and specified by Jeremiah, Josiah's ministering prophet.

The very length of these desolations – seventy years – was specified by this same prophet. Read Jer 29:10; 2 Chron 36:20-21. In the mind of anyone open to the voice of God there could be no doubt that they were in the last days of an age. God would move the seat of world rule from Jerusalem to Babylon, thus starting a period of Gentile world rule, the course and termination of which is outlined in Dan 2, 7, 9, 11. This period would run through the empires of Babylon, Medo-Persia, Greece, and Rome, all of which would be overthrown at the coming of Christ in glory to set up the kingdom of God on earth. It was a frightening time in which to live and one that could have frozen anyone into inaction, thinking that all was lost. But the man of God, who was king, must have been well aware of what the future held, since he was the friend and understudy of Jeremiah; he thought only of his duty to God, of the Lord's glory and the Lord's house.

3. Beginnings of Revival

There are many similarities between the revivals under Hezekiah and Josiah, and we shall not weary the reader with repetition of such parallels. There are also many differences, some of which are worthy of attention. Josiah came to the throne at the age of eight, and in his eighth year as king, when he was sixteen, he began to seek the God of his father David. We gather from this that the first step in revival is not making of plans and setting of goals, but a personal getting back to God in heart and a learning of His will through His word. Plans may be good and goals well considered, provided they are made in humility and dependence on God with a sense of one's own total inability to do anything for God apart from His help. This takes for granted what we have repeatedly stressed, that revival at any time must begin with heart condition rather than the reeling off of technical qualifications and human attainments. Genuine revival, as distinct from restructuring, starts with real brokenness before God, and a waiting on Him for the help and power of His Holy Spirit. There is a turning from our abilities, giftedness, or training, to God in His fulness to meet our need with warm hearts and devotion to Himself.

This is all embraced in the seeking of God. It is David's cry in Ps 63: "Early will I seek Thee; my soul thirsteth for Thee". Both are exemplified in Josiah. It is more than seeking God's will, God's help, God's knowledge – it is personal longing for God Himself and His communion. Josiah's finding of God at age twenty led to a burning desire to be done with everything and anything that would take God's place or compete with Him for the throne of the heart. And here we must remind ourselves that in a very subtle way things we never would consider as idols can be prominent in our thinking in the place of God, including our own capabilities. We can so easily exalt and make prominent things which are not at all outwardly like the ugly pagan idols. Man does so like to be important, but God must set him aside before He can start to do anything through him so that God might have the glory.

In the eighteenth year of his reign, when he would be twenty-six, Josiah began the great work of cleansing and restoring God's house and His worship. When this was done he could then lead in the celebration of passover and the other feasts. An early start in life was important, but it had to be followed by a consistent course of following God's will. He could not have known it, but he was to have only thirty-eight years of life altogether, i.e. twenty-two from the beginning of his work of revival. There is no time in our lives that we can afford to waste.

The long list of the idols and their temples which he destroyed shows the ground which had been lost for God in the previous two reigns. The thoroughness with which he proceeded shows his determination to do the job well whatever the cost. No half-way measures were tolerated where the Lord's supremacy was concerned, or obedience to His word was in question. The steps involve personal life and communion, devotion to God's truth, and then worship and service.

Chapter 13

Revival under Josiah: Rediscovery of the Scriptures

1. Finding the Book

IN all we have considered of revival it is obvious that God's word, either spoken or written, is central. To do anything for God we need directions from Him. We are not then surprised at what happened at this point in Josiah's experience even though *how* it happened may startle us.

Quite obviously one of the turning points in the story, and a very dramatic one, was the finding of the scroll of the Holy Scriptures in the temple while they were cleaning and restoring it. Commentators seem to take a lot of time and space discussing whether this was the original writing of Moses or a copy. Many authorities could be cited, but to no profit. It is clear that whether original or copy, they had lost in some very real sense the word of the Lord.

When Shaphan reads the books in the presence of the king, there is not only consternation, but shock and horror. The king tears his robe as a token of grief, and his words leave no doubt as to the cause. These are words which simply cry for our attention: "Go, inquire of the Lord for me and for them who are left in Israel and Judah, (the remnant) concerning the words of the book that is found, for great is the wrath of the Lord that is poured out on us because our fathers have not kept the word of the Lord, to do all that is written in this book". It seems that the teaching of the law had neither been known nor practised. Had they had copies but not the original, it would be hard to explain the apparent ignorance of their failure to keep all that was now known and seen to be "in the book". In view of the declared judgment of God against all departure from the written Word, their failure was a frightening thing. Whether they had been following oral instructions from the scribes and priests, or even tradition, is not clear. Hilkiah was a priest, and Shaphan a scribe, and they appear to have been as shocked as the king by what was in the book. We could weary ourselves in speculation and still miss the point: as a people they had lost the book of the law of the Lord.

2. Consequences of Losing the Book

We have already reminded ourselves of God's charge to Joshua in ch. 1 of that book, but a reference to it again will point up an important element in that command. The words are: "Be strong and very courageous, that thou mayest observe to do according to *all* the law which Moses my servant commanded thee." It was not merely a question of being guided in fundamental truths, or of conforming in a general way to God's law in major or spiritual matters only or in matters judged to be important, while in other matters using their own judgment. In our day we hear much of this; as long as we stick to the fundamentals, all other matters can be lumped together as those in which we are at liberty to do almost anything so long as it is not in conflict with "the fundamentals". Some then proceed to make their own little list of what is fundamental and what is not, and of course here there can be great diversity. In Joshua's life and leadership *all* the word of God had to be observed and obeyed, and God had gone on to say: "This book of the law shall not depart out of thy mouth; but thou shalt meditate therein day and night, that thou mayest observe to do according to *all* that is written therein." The orders are clear and any losing of the book must be seen as a major failure and the prelude to disaster.

When David was preparing to bring the ark of the covenant up to Jerusalem he reminded the priests and Levites of God's displeasure on their first attempt and of the discipline which this brought upon them in the words: "because we sought Him not after the due order" (1 Chron

15:13). There was an order for the lamps on the lampstand (Lev 24:4); orders in which the priests ministered; an order of offerings, of the set feasts of Jehovah, and of the parts of offerings and how they were to be placed on the altar. There was an order concerning the movement and transportation of the ark, as David learned at great cost. Any violation of God's order was visited with His displeasure, as on Aaron's sons with their strange fire, and on Uzziah for his intrusion into work which properly belonged to the priests.

In 1 Cor 14:40 the Spirit demands orderliness in the Lord's house; in Col 2:5 Paul rejoices when he sees the order in that congregation. The railer or the disorderly person has no place here. The mouth of the unruly and the gainsayer must be stopped; Titus is left for a time in Crete "to set in order the things that are lacking". In 1 Cor 11:16 in connection with the role and behaviour of the male and the female we have the plain words: "If any man seem to be contentious, we have no such custom, neither the churches of God". There was an accepted custom in the churches, obviously approved by God, and there was no room for a contentious person to force his personal opinions or exercise his "liberty" at the cost of disturbing the whole assembly.

Not only in fundamentals but in everything which pertains to the orderliness of God's house obedience is called for. 1 Timothy was written "that thou mightest know how thou oughtest behave thyself in the house of God". There is behaviour and order which is in keeping with that house. In Ps 119 the word of God is referred to under seven different titles, and the authority of God's word is seen in the psalm as applying to every part and phase of the life, whether personal, social, religious or whatever. It was departure from this total obedience in *all things* in Judges that brought failure and disaster. This was what impressed Josiah — not that some things might have been left out, but that they had not given complete fulfilment to *all that God* had commanded. The cause of all the disorder Josiah faced was that they had "lost the Book", a serious business indeed.

3. The Losing of the Book in the Church Age
a. The Apostolic Testimony

Looking back over church history it seems clear that one of the causes of departure was that of losing the authority of Holy Scripture. In apostolic times Timothy is urged to remember that the foundation of everything in his own life was "the sacred writings" which he had been taught from infancy, through which he had found the wisdom that leads to salvation, in which he had "faith", and which he had followed (1 Tim 1; 2 Tim 3:14-17). In these letters Timothy is ordered to charge and teach all he had learned and also to instruct systematically "faithful men who shall be able to teach others also". Timothy was to see that those appointed as overseers were "apt (competent) to teach", and Titus in similar instructions is told that such men must "hold fast the faithful word as [they] have been taught", so that they in turn might be able to give "sound teaching" to others (Titus 1:9). The warning is that in coming times men would not put up with sound teaching but would seek teachers of a more acceptable kind who would titillate the itching ears and jaded tastes of their hearers (2 Tim 4).

By contrast they were to be "stablished in the faith as ye have been taught . . . [and] beware lest any man spoil (rob) you through philosophy and vain deceit after the rudiments (basics) of the world" (Col 2:7-8). Last days would be characterised by "departing from the faith", but the "good servant of Jesus Christ" is to be nourished up in the "words of the faith and of sound (healthful) teaching" (1 Tim 4:6).

These and many other NT passages make it clear that God's people, whether individually or collectively, were to be governed at every level of life and practice by Holy Scripture alone. John's epistles, among the very latest books of the Bible, have the word "truth" or "the truth" some seventeen times and if we add John's Gospel we have a total of forty occurrences, which is as many as all other NT writers combined. John would remember this as he recorded in ch. 17 of his Gospel that the Lord had said: "Thy word is truth". In Timothy Paul refers to those who "never come to the knowledge of the truth", to others who have "erred from the truth", to some who turn the ears of others "away from the truth" and yet again "resist the truth". All this is sadly true of what actually happened.

b. The Post-Apostolic Period

A short time after the apostles, church history shows the inroads of many changes. From a number of overseers in one local church, as seen in Acts 20:28, we see one man taking over "the care" of a local church. Then came one man becoming "bishop" of a number of churches in an area, and later archbishops or patriarchs of whole countries. Gradually great church leaders appear who handed down instructions and edicts for the churches. Bit by bit, the Word was lost so far as a sense of its total authority was concerned, and the Dark Ages set in May there be significance in the fact that the word "leaders", a very popular word in our day, seems totally absent in the NT except for the Lord's denunciation of "blind leaders of the blind"?

In those dark ages all sorts of developments, accretions, and arrangements were introduced: admission to the church by baptism, infant baptism, a structuring of "the church" on the administrative patterns of the Roman Empire with laity and clergy, and orders already described, human ordinations and consecrations to church "offices and authority", joining of church and state etc. The writings of "the Fathers" took the place of Holy Scripture until some centuries later the Roman church wound up with saints, purgatory, confession, a Pope, the Mass, an intermediary priesthood, celibacy, indulgences, Mariolatry etc. and all because it had for all practical purposes "lost the book". The words and traditions of men not only took the place of the Bible, but most of the clergy were almost totally ignorant of the Bible itself. Its possession by the laity was forbidden and few others cared about it. Those who first attempted to translate it into the language of the people were persecuted and in many cases burned as heretics.

c. The Bible and the Reformation

"*Sola Scriptura*" (The Scriptures alone), one of the battlecries of the Reformation, was a mighty wind blowing across the professing church and the world, and the translating, printing, and circulating of the Bible began, with all its liberating, enlightening, and purifying power. The Book, lost for many centuries, was again found, though even then not obeyed in all things or to the limit. Many anti-scriptural practices were carried over from the ages of darkness. Churches remained made up of converted and unconverted; they held on to baptism of infants for admission, hierarchical clerical structures, linking of the church with the secular power, etc.

d. Attacks on the Authority of Scripture

Because of the great restoration of much truth which had swept the church through the rediscovery of the Scriptures and their widespread distribution and preaching, it is not surprising that Satan should attack from many angles. There was the sceptic, the agnostic, the atheist, the evolutionist on the one hand, and the liberal modernist, the higher critic, the ritualist who either put the church above the Bible or in practice put the rubrics or constitution alongside it. In one way or another all worked to undermine the authority of a divinely-unique and God-breathed Scripture. In this way not only our society but also many churches have in effect ignored, bypassed, or thrown out the Bible – they have lost it again! Of course from the very beginning there were groups in almost all periods, of various sizes and with varying degrees of light and knowledge of Scripture, who protested and even revolted against and separated from the mainline corruption. Most of them met with fierce persecution and most of their own works have been destroyed while all sorts of false reports have been spread about their beliefs and practices. We recommend the reading of E.H. Broadbent's *The Pilgrim Church*, a classic on the subject.

In more recent times there have been many protests against departure from the Scriptures, and many separations from what could no longer be influenced or changed when it reached unacceptable limits. There is no lack of Bibles in our day, or of good commentaries on them for that matter, but the Bible can be lost in more ways than simply mislaying the printed book. One of the movements above referred to and sometimes called for convenience "the brethren movement" took place among men who were well acquainted with the letter of the Scriptures even in the original languages, but many things taught in those Scriptures were not finding expression in their church-life because the teachings of men had come in to supersede them. When the word of God gripped their hearts in this new way, demanding that they return to its simplicity, they obeyed without hesitation, though in many cases it cost them much. It has been claimed in recent years that these people were not guided by "doctrine", indeed that doctrine became very much secondary, since the chief driving force of their movement was love and fellowship. The kindest construction one can put on this is that those who say such things have either not read the writings of the people they are discussing, or else they have totally misunderstood them.

One of the men of that movement, H.W. Soltau, has written a little booklet trying to explain what really was their aim and what influenced them. The booklet, entitled *They found it written*, from first to last is the story of men who searched the Scriptures with great diligence and were so driven that, as they found something which had been lost to them, they immediately starting following it. It was a burning desire to give fulfilment to what they found that drew them together – not sentiment nor emotion though there was probably enough of that, but *truth*. It is the thesis of the present writer, that true revival will always spring from obedience to God's word, and will produce more obedience to that Word.

Chapter 14

Josiah: The Results of Finding the Book

1. Far-reaching Benefits

EVERYTHING which followed the recovery of the word of God in Josiah's day is said to flow from that fact. All hearts and consciences were touched by the book and its teaching; everyone was humbled and obedient, for the king, along with a few of the more prominent men, was not content to know the Word himself. He gathered all into Jerusalem and there the book was read to them, with its commandments, testimonies, and statutes applied. We have already explained that the law of God comprised these three sections, their relation to every phase of an Israelite's life. They are solemnly charged to get back to the fulfilling of this law and indeed all entered into a covenant to do this, "and all his days they departed not from following the Lord, the God of their fathers" 2 Chron 34: 33. All this signifies a return to the constant teaching of the Word.

As in Hezekiah's days one of the first things grasped was that the gatherings of God's people should be conscientiously kept; passover and unleavened bread. No doubt, since it occurred at the same time they would include the sheaf of firsfruits as well. All was sone "as it is written in the book of Moses."

At the same time Josiah instructed the Levites to "put the holy ark in the house which Solomon son of David king of Israel did build; it shall not be a burden on your shoulders" (2 Chron 35:3). The ark is said in both Romans and Hebrews to be a type or figure of Christ. True revival will be careful to put Him in His proper place among His people in fulfilment of God's instructions. This is a touching reference, since it would appear from the wording

98

that during at least the fifty-seven years of Manasseh and Amon when the temple was plundered and defiled, unused and abandoned, faithful men had removed the ark of the covenant to safety, guarding it from all harm and carrying it from place to place on their shoulders which was the God-ordained way for its transportation. There were always faithful hearts totally devoted to what spoke of Christ and aware that the covenant which bound them to God was important. The mercy seat was where the blood was sprinkled in atonement for their sins, overshadowed by the golden cherubim, the guardians or upholders of the holiness of God. All was significant and sacred so they made the guarding of it their responsibility. Because of surrounding ignorance and desolation, this must have been a thankless job as far as men were concerned and, at times, even a dangerous one. However dark the days God would always have a remnant in faithfulness.

This remnant no doubt included Hilkiah, Shaphan, Huldah, and the names given in 35:8-9. And may we not say that Josiah's mother Jedidah was one of the company? And Jeremiah and Zephaniah? It was through this remnant, including many many others also, who had guarded the ark in the darkness, that the work of the revival was moved forward. Such people are needed by God if there is to be genuine revival in our days. We are told that there had been kept in Israel no passover like this since the days of Samuel, nor any of the kings who followed his times. So the greatest passover of the whole of the kingdom period was kept in a time of darkness and weakness, and almost at the end of the age!

2. A Sad Conclusion

In the very last days of Josiah's wonderful life by one act of inexplicable folly this great man lost his life at thirty-nine years of age. He meddled in something which was none of his business. Assyria was a great power by this time and had taken Syria as well as other possessions from Egypt. Pharaoh Necho decided to get himself some glory by attacking and recovering some of this territory, one of his targets being the great citadel and city of Carchemish on the Euphrates. He was passing through the northern part of Israel, which was largely dependent on him, with no intention of harassing its inhabitants, when Josiah decided for some strange reason to influence world affairs. It is hard to understand what could have led him into such a blunder. At thirty-nine years of age his whole life had been taken up with internal affairs of Israel, and there is no hint that he had any experience in war, or any special genius for it. But even supposing he had, it was never God's will that His people should become involved in the affairs of the surrounding nations, much less interfere in their wars.

Note Abraham's position in the highlands with God while nine petty kings fought in the valley of the slimepits, and contrast it with Lot's who had managed to become a senator in Sodom, only to wind up a prisoner-of-war on his way to some slave market in the Euphrates valley. It was all written for our learning.

Poor Josiah was warned by God, through the mouth of the pagan Pharaoh, not to meddle in affairs which did not concern him, but he insisted and was cut down. Was he carried away by his success in spiritual things, seeing himself as more important and powerful than he really was? Or was he deluded into thinking that he could somehow tinker with the balance of power between the two empires? Or was he seeking to ingratiate himself with Assyria and so postpone the day of Israel's judgment? Certain it is that he failed, and that he had not seen matters from God's viewpoint; indeed Babylon and not Assyria was to be the ultimate foe.

Josiah was swept contemptuously aside and Necho went on in triumph, taking Carchemish and returning via Jerusalem where he deposed Josiah's son Jehoahaz and carried him to

Egypt (where he died). Necho then put his brother Eliakim on the throne in his place, changing his name to Jehoiakim. He also laid on Israel a tribute of one hundred talents of silver and one talent of gold, a talent being over a hundred pounds weight.

God thus set aside all pretensions of the flesh to be able to further His work or purposes. Instead of His people being helped by the flesh, it only made things worse and hastened the dissolution. Read 2 Kings 23:29-34; 2 Chron 35:20-24; Jer 26:20-23, as well as the end of 2 Kings and 2 Chron. It is a depressing end to a story of decline and departure but one, we feel sure, from which we are intended to learn something.

Chapter 15

Back From Babylon

1. Ezra and Nehemiah

AS we turn to the books of Ezra and Nehemiah and the great revival brought about through their influence, more than seventy years had rolled by. These years had brought the sorrows and devastation of Nebuchadnezzar's invasions and the deportation of many, perhaps most, of the middle and upper classes to Babylon. There they remained throughout the seventy years of "the desolations" predicted by Jeremiah. (Read Jer 25:9-12, 29:10; 2 Chron 36: 17-21.) As that period of discipline under God's hand drew to a close there was a stir in the hearts of many who had kept the flame of hope and loyalty alight during all the years of darkness.

The revival recorded in these two books, which are always considered by the Jewish people as one and have been always so marked in their Bible, is one of the most thrilling of the whole Bible. So many books have been written about it in detail that it would be folly to try write anything new on the subject. Our aim is quite different. We wish simply to focus attention on the basic spiritual principles underlying this great movement of God.

This was more than a revival; it was a return to their homeland, a repossessing of a sacred heritage given them by God, but from which they had been torn in God's judgment on their sin. It was coming back to where God had always wanted them to be, a re-entry into the land of God's providing and to participation in His purposes which they had lost through disobedience and departure from His word. This is the story of their return to both the land and the word in order to rebuild the place in which God could dwell. He would be able to find all His delight in being among them and rejoicing in their obedience and devotion. Recovery was accomplished when they were at their weakest, with nothing in themselves to which they could look for success. May we not learn something from this right on the threshold of the whole study?

The land speaks to us of the place of our inheritance also, the heavenlies of Eph 1 which God intends us to enter, possess, cultivate, and enjoy. Unfortunately, we are so often strangers there, at least experientially. Whether through carelessness or neglect we lose our enjoyment of this heavenly inheritance; we then can expect nothing but the discipline of God. The path back, in our case as in that of Israel in this story, follows the same course.

There are great differences of opinion even among specialists regarding the chronology and also the sequence of events in the the two books. Some put fifty to sixty years between the several migrations from Babylon to Jerusalem. Some would alter the order of these migrations. Some see the whole of the two books as parallel reports of the same period which completely overlap; others see them as overlapping only during certain periods. There are also some very knowledgeable experts who say that the generally accepted chronology of the whole period is in error by many years due to mistakes by other experts! Need we say that there are experts on all sides of all these opinions?

This book will not go into any of these arguments since we are seeking the spiritual principles which underlie spiritual revival and restoration, rather than dates and chronologies, important though they are. These two books are full of spiritual lessons which do not require detailed knowledge of all the dates, though some time factors are clear and precise.

2. The Desolations of Jerusalem

It must be understood that the Babylonians invaded Israel three times in those last days of the monarchy, but only in the final invasion were the city and the temple completely destroyed. At that point the "desolations" began which were to last for seventy years (see 2 Chron 36:21). Three puppet kings were set up during this period of the invasions: Jehoiakim, Jehoiachin, and Zedekiah, the first and last of whose names were given them by their conquerors and overlords. During this period the prophet Jeremiah, who had been left in the land, prophesied that they would spend seventy years in exile, and would then be allowed to return (Jer 25:9-11; 29:10). But many years before any of this happened Isaiah had delivered a message from the Lord: "Who (God is the subject) saith of Cyrus, 'He is my shepherd, and shall perform all my pleasure; even saying to Jerusalem. Thou shalt be built; and to the temple, thy foundation shall be laid'". And so it happened, for we read in Ezra 1: "In the first year of Cyrus king of Persia, that the word of the Lord by the mouth of Jeremiah might be fulfilled, the Lord stirred up the spirit of Cyrus king of Persia saying ... the Lord God of heaven ... hath charged me to build a house at Jerusalem. The edict goes on to say that all who were willing to go to their land for this purpose were free to do so, and the king also gave them back "the vessels of the house of the Lord" so that they could take them back to Israel for the new temple.

It is also to be noted that the whole business was based on God's working in men and through men, indeed overruling in everything. Not only so but this was seen, felt, and acknowledged to be so by those involved. Ezra 1:1 reads: "The Lord stirred up the spirit of Cyrus king of Persia"; v.5 of the same chapter states clearly that from top to bottom of those who shared in this great movement it belonged to "all those whose spirit God had raised, to go up to build the house of the Lord which is in Jerusalem". This was no mere plan or philosophy worked out by a few and then "sold" to the mass. It was in every sense a work of God the Holy Spirit. Ringing like a chime throughout both books are words like "according to the good hand of my God upon me", "I was strengthened as the hand of my God was upon me", "Hear, Oh our God, for we are despised", "My God, think upon me" . . . These men saw neither strength nor ability in themselves, but their faith was strong in God, and they were fully convinced that with Him they had "no lack". They were also very conscious of the word of God which had promised that after seventy years of desolations they could and would come back to their position of blessing. (Read Jer 25:9-12; 29:10; 2 Chron 36: 17-21; Dan 9:2.) They were responding to God's grace as revealed in His word with no dependence on their own abilities or expertise or planning. We would be wise to learn from them.

3. The Men God Used
a. The Cost of Returning
As we have seen, many hearts were stirred by God, but the number of those who volunteered was small when compared with the numbers who did not. Ezra gives the number of those who went up in the first migration with Zerubbabel as 42,360 to which were added 7,337 servants of various classes, for a total of just under 50,000 in round numbers. We are told that many had done well in Babylon, especially after the empire fell to the Medes and Persians. Abba Eban, an Israeli statesman and historian, has said that many had become wealthy and established as traders, bankers and landowners. It is easy to believe that such types would have little taste for going back to a life of hardship in a desolate land to build the house of the Lord and begin afresh facing opposition from settlers who had been brought in to take their place. The number mentioned is a tiny minority, indeed they are called "a remnant of the people". It was obviously not a national reorganisation but a movement of heart and spirit in those who were touched by God.

The names of the leaders involved are full of instruction. They were great-hearted spiritual giants prepared to give up a life of comfort in a land tainted by sin and idolatry, yet where under an obviously benevolent government many had prospered and so were determined to remain. Some of the Israelitish leaders are worth a little notice. At the time of the Babylonish invasion God had in grace put three key men of spiritual stature in places of His choice. Ezekiel was put among the captives by the river Chebar in Babylon (Ezek 1:1). Daniel was placed as a young man in the conqueror's palace where he continued until the time of this very Cyrus and indeed functioned as his counsellor (Dan 6:28). Daniel also saw to it that his three devoted companions were promoted (Dan 2:49; 3:30). But at the same time God had left Jeremiah in Israel with the poorer class people who had been left behind at the time of the deportation. Thus the Lord saw to it that in the desolate land of Israel, among the exiles in the slave camps and in the palace, He had His witnesses, who with others no doubt, taught and kept the fire of God burning in many hearts, awaiting God's day at the end of the seventy years. None of them had an easy place but each accepted it as from God and occupied it for God's glory in his own measure.

They were not alone for we read in the book of Esther of a lonely but valiant Mordecai who braved every danger to stand up for God and His people. It is interesting to note that there is a Mordecai mentioned among the leaders of the first wave of those who returned to the land with Nehemiah and Zerubbabel in Ezra 2:2. Whether he was the same or a relative we have no way of knowing, but the name is there. Their masters had in some cases changed their names to those of their pagan gods and put pressure on them, even to dens of lions and roaring furnaces, to conform and assimilate – but they stoutly resisted and remained faithful to the word of God.

b. Different Men for Different Jobs

As well as those we have mentioned there were others whose names figured prominently in this great revival as is well known: Nehemiah, Zerubbabel, Ezra, Jeshua or Joshua, Haggai, and Zechariah. They filled different positions, and were obviously men of very different talents, Zerubbabel as govenor, Jeshua as high priest, Ezra as teacher, Nehemiah as leader, exhorter, and on occasion as energetic headknocker, while Haggai and Zechariah were prophets sent to urge the people on in times of defeat, depression, laziness, and self-serving materialism. (Read Haggai 1.) Not only were they in different positions with different gifts and jobs, but were ever men less alike in personality and character? Zerubbabel is a prince of the royal line of David and heir to the throne of Israel as the fourth generation descendant of Josiah, the last real king of the nation. Of Nehemiah we know nothing except the name of his father, and that he had a brother Hanani who preceded him to Israel and brought back word of the suffering there (Neh 1:2). Jeshua is high priest, but Ezra is only a priest though much more notable, as we shall see, as a Bible teacher, indeed the prototype and model for Bible teachers of all time.

Even the two prophets sent to stimulate the people, and whose messages are preserved for us in the books bearing their names, could not have been less alike in their ministry. Zechariah soars in a poetic style not inferior to Isaiah, and certainly not less majestic or moving. He lifts them to action in the building of the house of God by giving them word paintings of the great millennial temple to be built by the coming priest-king (of whom Jeshua is but a picture, Zech 6:11-14). Haggai, on the other hand, though ministering at the same time, has a style all his own; as an exhorter he scolds, tongue-lashes, skewers them with scornful irony about their panelled homes while God's house lies in weed-covered ruin. He lampoons them as making much of their expensive clothing when in fact they remind him of shivering beggars whose rags neither keep out cold nor keep in heat; they are busy making money but forget that it is being put into in bags full of holes. Anyone who preached like this even once among us would surely never be invited back since it might offend some of our very respectable meeting-attenders in the comfortable pews.

Are we to suppose that one of these preachers was better than the other, or that one might better have copied the tactics of the other, or modelled his preaching style on that of his colleague?

And what shall we say about the contrast between gentle Jeshua who had trouble even disciplining his own family (Neh 13:4, 28) and Nehemiah who argued, reasoned, stormed, commanded, and, when all else failed, shook some rascals by the beard and knocked their heads together! God uses all kinds and is sovereign not only in His choice but also in making men the way they are in the first place. Read Jer 1:5; "Before I formed thee in the belly I knew thee, and before thou camest forth out of the womb I sanctified thee and I ordained thee a prophet and . . . thou shalt go . . ."

Although so different, yet they worked together in a common task, the rebuilding of God's dwelling once brought to ruin by their nation's disobedience and departure from God. They worked and there is no record of disagreement or friction among them. We greatly fear that some of these dear men in our day would have failed the tests of "discipling", "leadership training courses", "philosophy of ministry" and "neighbourhood strategies" in order to obtain letters of commendation and support.

In a spiritual sense our task is similar, since God's temple and dwelling on earth is the church, and since that dwelling-place is to-day in a sad condition, we must note the warning. "Let every man take heed how he buildeth" (1 Cor 3:9-17). These men and women had a job to do; clearing away the rubbish and rubble and building. We also have a sobering responsibility, and there is much clearing of the ground to be done too.

Chapter 16

Revival of the Exile: a Divine Work

1. Early stirrings

AS we have seen, God began by stirring the heart of Cyrus; in the same chapter we read of those "whose spirit the Lord had raised". This was no spur-of-the-moment decision by a group of enthusiasts urged on by specialists in renewal. God had said that Israel would spend seventy years in the desolations (2 Chron 36:20-21) because for 490 years they had not allowed the land to rest one year in seven as He had commanded. They had robbed God's land of seventy years of rest and it would now lie fallow and uncultivated for that period. If at the end of that time they turned in heart to God, He would answer and bring them back.

The first move on their part would have to be of the heart. Dan 9 says: "I Daniel understood by [the] books the number of the years, whereof the word of the Lord came to Jeremiah the prophet that He would accomplish seventy years in the desolations of Jerusalem. And I set my face unto the Lord God to seek by prayer and supplications with fasting ..." Ezekiel had been told by special messenger the very date and day of the final invasion and destruction of Jerusalem so that the completion of the seventy years could be accurately calculated (Ezek 33:21-22). Isaiah had mentioned the name of the king who would be the instrument. Now all is ready, the time has come, the man is on the throne, and God's prophetic promise will be fulfilled. One is tempted to wonder why God, who is sovereign, did not raise up the spirit of everyone to leave Babylon, and go back to the land of promise. In this we must remember that God rarely uses conscripts; that the king had sent out a challenge in 1:3 saying: "Who is there

among you of all His people ... let him go up to Jerusalem."
The call was there, but many may have been so engrossed
in the attractions of the land of their exile that the building
of a dwelling-place and a witness for God had little appeal,
especially in a barren and hostile surrounding full of
enemies and mockers? Unfortunately, such sentiments are
all too common even in our own day; many are called but
few are chosen. Some are wrought upon by the Holy Spirit
as His call goes out, but they are either too far from Him
even to hear the call, or too insensitive to His interests to
bother or think it worth while. We simply must believe that
God would have wished all His children back in His land,
but only fifty thousand out of possibly millions responded
to His desire.

2. The first group returns to the land

In Ezra 1 Cyrus sends out the call and immeditely a band
of God's people who had been longing for the day, respond
and set out for the land which they had lost through
departure from God. Among those responsive to the call of
God was Zerubbabel, the great-grandson of Josiah, leader
of the last great revival. By his side was Jeshua the high
priest. Godly parents had instilled the Scriptures into the
minds of their offspring; in time it bore fruit. The old saint
Daniel, counsellor to Cyrus, is seen bowed over the sacred
writings regarding the promised return, and pouring out
his heart in repentance, confession and supplication, not
only for himself but for "thy people" (Dan 9).

This old man Daniel must be seen as one of the clearest
links between the deportation of the past and the revival of
the present. Were he, and perhaps his faithful companions
in the captivity, now old men, the teachers of this new
generation? Like Caleb and Joshua, had they kept
alight the fires of hope and devotion to their God in the
darkest of days? The very name of Zerubbabel ("seed of
Babylon") indicates that he had been born in the captivity
and we may assume that most of his companions would

have been also, with the exception, of course, of Daniel and some of his younger companions.

There will always be living links of godly souls who, however sad the days and discouraging the circumstances, will continue to stand for God's truth and teach it to the oncoming generations, particularly to their own children. Some may encourage their children to depart from the truth simply because there are not enough young people in the assembly or because they consider the meetings dull, their needs are not being met and their talents are "not being used". If we were to apply these standards to the people of God in the Babylonish captivity and note the manner in which the faithful ones responded to God's "stirring", it would put us to shame. Would they have refused to go back to God because of lack of young people, or because there would be so little to attract those who had cultivated a taste for the brighter world of Babylon? In Babylon there was more for their children. But these people were made of sterner stuff and had taught their children the value of shaping their lives by God's word rather than by the surrounding lifestyle of Babylon. God had spoken; the time had come; they would return to their Biblical roots.

God's care in preserving in the inspired Word the very names and numbers of those who "went up" in Ezra 2 warms our hearts by the thought that He knows the name of every one willing to move forward with Him. He puts each one into the place He has chosen for them and gives them the work for which He has prepared them. It is also to be noted that as well as the people being named individually as cared for by God, their animals and possessions, down to the humblest donkey, are all evaluated and recorded by Him. Not surprisingly there was a response to God; there was a willing contribution in gold and silver (money) for the actual building of the house, and this began with the leaders, "the chiefs of the fathers' houses", an example which would later be followed by all – they would give of their ability (Ezra 2:69). The leaders did not tell the people what to do but rather by doing it provided models for the people to imitate. (See 1 Pet 5:3 where the word rendered "example" is really "model".)

The closing verses of the chapter inform us that each tribe, clan, and house went back to their own allotted place which had been designated for them centuries before according to God's plan under Joshua. There was no confusion or seeking of a place other than that given them by their God.

3. The Gathering to Jerusalem to Set Up the Altar.
a. Setting up the altar

We learn from later passages that the city walls, and probably homes, were in ruin; yet the repairing of these was not their first concern; rebuilding their homes would be seen to in its proper time. The altar must come first. When "the altar" is mentioned without further qualification it seems always to speak of the altar of burnt offering, also called "the great altar," and "the altar of the Lord" and "the brazen altar". In Malachi 1:7, 12 this altar is referred to as God's table and what was offered on it is there called His food. The sacrifices offered thereon spoke of a coming Christ on whose perfections the Father could feast His heart with complete delight. It was at this altar in both tabernacle and temple, placed as it was at the entrance door, that all worship and approach to God must begin.

The returned Israelites were therefore determined that this altar with all that it meant should come first. Not their military security, not their homes, not their plans for organisation or reorganisation, and not what *they* would get out of it, but that which would satisfy the heart and affections of God was uppermost in their minds. One wonders when we are going to learn that worship must come before everything else? "Thou shalt worship the Lord thy God" is the first and prime commandment, and if it adds, "and Him only shalt thou serve", the Lord Himself interprets this for us in Matt 4:10 as priestly service, the same word for priestly service which is used throughout Hebrews of the service of the priests, and indeed in Rev 7:15; 22:3 in connection with the redeemed in heaven.

Worship is the expression of devotion, and of our appreciation of what Christ is to the Father and then to us. It is above and beyond praise and thanksgiving, both of which are appropriate and can be ingredients and expressions of worship. A moment's consideration will convince us that we both praise and thank people whom we have no thought of worshipping. It is worth remembering also, that worship is not even being taken up with the blessings and benefits which have come to us in Christ. These are more associated with praise and thanksgiving. We tend to be self-centred in occupation with what Christ has done for us rather than what He means to the Father and has done for Him and His glory.

Worship is not merely another meeting, but is distinct from all other gatherings in that it is one in which we give to God rather than getting from God or learning about God, or even praying to God. It is the highest activity of the Christian and therefore calls for the highest spiritual condition. Worship is therefore the spiritual barometer of any assembly, and since all else flows from our appreciation of the Lord, when worship is flawed, neglected, or displaced by anything, there can be no true revival. The servant who was condemned for lack of proper service in the parable of the talents failed in service because of His low appreciation of his master, "I knew thee that thou art a hard man."

These people in Ezra's day did not even build the temple first, but the altar where God could get what He longed for from His people. This is specifically said to be in obedience to the word of God as delivered by Moses. The first step in true revival is obedience to the Word in giving worship priority over everything else.

b. Offerings and feasts

The altar in itself was not enough; they offered burnt offerings on it morning and evening, what is called the "continual burnt offering". Neither sin offerings nor trespass offerings are mentioned yet, and neither of these was ever offered on this altar, they were burnt with fire outside the camp. The burnt offering is a picture of Christ offering Himself to the Father in death for a sweet savour and apart entirely from sin. It is the highest aspect of worship, and what a blessed experience this must have been to the Israelites re-established in God's land! They had never, and could never, have done this in Babylon nor anywhere else in the world since there was neither temple not altar there, much less a functioning priesthood, or sacrifices considered clean by God.

God had forbidden these offerings to be offered anywhere else than "where He had chosen to place His name" (Deut 26:2). That place was later stated by God to be Jerusalem, and that is why our passage says that they "gathered themselves together as one man to Jerusalem." The gathering together of God's people is not only a precious blessing to them in many ways, but is also precious to God, and indeed commanded by Him. This preciousness is easily explained when we understand that the gathering of His people is said to be "unto Him". Israel was put under a solemn charge and on pain of being "cut off" to gather themselves together (the males particularly) at Jerusalem at least three times each year. The subject of these and other gatherings is rich in its spiritual teaching, even for us, but this cannot be more than touched on in this brief study. But beyond all else these "feasts of Jehovah" were to honour Him, while to absent oneself was the very opposite. Read Lev 23; Num 28; Deut 16. 1 Cor 5:7

connects all with the present age.

Attention is drawn to the fact that even the foundation of the temple of the Lord was not yet laid (3:6), yet in anticipation of this and with nothing material but the altar, and counting alone on the presence of the Lord, they poured out their all in an ecstasy of joy. How much like this is a company in our day with little of outward glory or even strength, just meeting around the altar in His name in a day of breakdown. They gather to Him alone and count on His presence. These are the very first steps toward revival.

Chapter 17

Revival after the Exile: Laying the Foundation

1. Necessary preparations

THOUGH the laying of the foundation was only in the second year after they had reached Jerusalem, the time between was not wasted. During it they were pouring out their offerings not only on the altar to God but also in money and food and drink to craftsmen of Tyre and Sidon for the bringing down of cedar wood to be used in the building of the temple. It was costly and hard work which could not be rushed, for all must be done according to God's plan as we see from v. 10b. It ws not what was convenient, quick, or in line with some self-set goals. Much less were they thinking about something more up-to-date or contemporary with a little bit of Babylonish or Egyptian architecture to make it more acceptable to the surrounding nations or to attract bigger audiences.

The pattern was to be followed, though we can easily picture the long hours, and probably months, which they spent in poring over the Sacred Writings, discussing, praying, seeking advice and guidance from those best qualified to explain each point before drawing up their plans according to what they had read. It would not come easily for, as we have seen, most of these men had been born in captivity where there was no temple, no functioning priesthood and probably only limited freedom to teach such things. Their only guide or source of information about the building of the temple was the word of God.

There was another problem in that they had been obliged to speak the language of their conquerors and gradually accepted and adapted that language to their own uses.

There are suggestions that some at least of the people spoke this Western Aramaic, a Semitic language originally from Aram or Mesopotamia, the land of the Euphrates. So it is likely that the mass of the less educated people born in Babylon would have had difficulty with the old Hebrew Scriptures. Later on in Neh 8 the teacher Ezra read from the Scriptures and then "gave the sense" because of the prevailing ignorance of Hebrew in which the original text was written.

All this would no doubt complicate their enquiry. Possibly they required interpreters and long hours of explanation and study, but no price was too high to pay. They were determined not to follow prevailing styles in the surrounding society, but to do everything according to the word of the Lord.

It is important that we learn the lesson which has been taught us by every revival which we can study whether Biblical or in more recent times namely: that revival comes by way of a return to obedience to God's word and never by disobeying or bypassing it. It would be a strange thing indeed to imagine that we can get back to God by disobeying Him or neglecting His instructions!

We have urged earlier that we keep in mind the fact that God's purpose and activity in this age is to "build His church", which church is His temple. The people of Ezra's day were building His dwelling and we are engaged in the same work. The church is more than a mission hall; it is the sanctuary, the dwelling place of God, a fact which many seem to have been forgotten. Holiness and order, His order, are essential in His house if He is to dwell there. At the consecration of the temple in 2 Chron 7 "The glory of the Lord filled the house" but when they defiled it, filling it with their disorder and corruption He departed from it (Ezek 10, 11). A short time later all was destroyed and they were deported. The book of the covenant, the ark where it was kept, and the tabernacle covering it were all said to be "the testimony". The church is, in itself and by His glory and order, His testimony in this age: "That now unto the principalities and powers in heavenly places might be known by the church the manifold wisdom of God, according to the eternal purpose which He purposed in Christ Jesus our Lord" (Eph 3:10-11). We do not preach to principalities and powers in heavenly places; we show them by the order and holiness of His house.

2. Laying the foundation

When the foundation was laid, no doubt small and surrounded by ruins on every hand, a strange thing happened. The "ancient men" wept, while the younger people "shouted aloud for joy" (Ezra 3:12), and the people could not distinguish which was which. Was one group right and one wrong? Small beginnings in the midst of much deadness and failure and surrounded by the marks of God's displeasure because of our sins will always bring a sense of pain and humiliation to those who remember better things. But those exercised souls who have not experienced these better things will be filled with joy. The two can, and do, go together betimes, sorrow and shame for our failure, and yet joy that something is being done because "the good hand of our God is upon us".

Chapter 18

Revival after the Exile: Enemies in Action

1. Offers of collaboration

FOUNDATIONS are important, but in themselves they are not enough. There is danger in being so attached to foundations that we do not advance much beyond them. We are exhorted in Heb 6:1 to "go on to full growth ... not laying again the foundation ..." This regathered people of God were determined to go beyond foundations and to build. Here they came up against opposition of a very powerful sort. God never does a work that Satan will not attack with all his craftiness and guile. The proof of this lies on the surface from Gen 3 to Rev 20:7-8. And so it was with this revival and indeed with all the revivals. In Ezra 4, 5 we have quite a few names involved in such opposition. We need not be occupied with their names since they do not turn up again in the present history. Their tactics, however, are of interest since they have been used from age to age.

First they asked to be allowed to join in the work, a suggestion that was promptly declined. The approach was subtle, professing oneness of devotion to a common God whom, they say, they had worshipped since the days of Esar-Haddon, king of Assyria. In a measure this was true, but it was not the whole truth and this is often the worst of lies.

When the ten northern tribes were defeated and many of them deported, the Assyrians, fearing to allow the land to lie largely uninhabited, imported masses of various pagan nations to settle in these areas. The history recorded in 2 Kings 17 shows that at first they simply continued in idolatry as they had always done, but as wild animals increased in the land, in their superstitious fear they

120

decided to find out something of "the manner of the God of the land". They appealed to the king who had sent them there, and he in turn sent them some of the priests who "taught them how they should fear the Lord."

A serious flaw in all this was the fact that these priests were not of the line of Aaron, nor were they in any sense priests of God. They were descended from those "ordained" by the rebel king Jeroboam from among the rabble and put in charge of the worship of the golden calves which that king had set up at the northern and southern limits of his kingdom specifically to keep his people from going to Jerusalem to worship, as all Israelites were commanded to do. What this led to is outlined in the last few verses of this chapter of 2 Kings: "So they feared the Lord, and made unto themselves of the lowest of them priests of the high places, who sacrificed for them in the houses of the high place. They feared the Lord and served their own gods after the manner of the nations whence they had been carried away."

These are the people who now ask to be taken into the work of rebuilding the house of Jehovah, but before they present their proposition the Holy Spirit calls them "the adversaries", and with spiritual perception the people of God see them as such and turn down their offer. The reply is unequivocal: "You have nothing to do with us to build a house unto our God . . . we ourselves together will build unto the Lord God of Israel". Satan knows well that his servants can work much more successfully from the inside than the outside.

There are at least four lessons for us here, and we do well to pay heed to them:

1. In any work for God spiritual perception is very important, that we may be able to distinguish between the true and false. Lack of such perception seems to be a great weakness in many who are in positions of oversight in assemblies to-day and, we believe, the root

of many of our problems. There seems a woeful lack of alertness to what may be involved in the new policies or where some of these suggestions and philosophies may lead. If they appear helpful, or maybe an answer to our problems, or even successful, showing results in other places, then too many are ready to accept any new thing which may be plausibly presented to them. Yet in Titus 1 the overseer must be one who "holds fast the faithful word as he has been taught, the he may be able by sound teaching both to exhort and confute the opposers". These opposers would be the adversaries of Nehemiah's day, but to confute them we must first be able to recognise them for what they truly are. The shepherd of the flock who would stand between the wolf and the sheep (John 10) must first be able to recognise a wolf when he sees one.

2. Having recognised these men as adversaries the Israelites had the courage to confront them with the truth. Moral courage is one of the basic characteristics of a true shepherd, and one which, alas, is sometimes in short supply.

3. The Israelites knew what "the truth" was, for they were well versed in it. Again there is great lack of Bible study and knowledge in the places where today it is most needed.

4. God's word teaches us that God's work must be done by God's people with no imported helpers from the enemy and no financial support from them either. The world, the flesh, and the devil are all enemies of God and His work, and if allowed, will hinder or destroy the building. In relating this to our own instruction we are not at all likening these men to our brethren in Christ. They were not brethren of the Israelites; they were aliens, adversaries, and proved themselves to be determined enemies though they first came with enticing offers of partnership and help. We must keep in mind what has

already been urged in these pages that there is a
religious world as well as a social and a political one, and
that they are equally antagonistic to God's work in this
age. Yet we are frequently told that we can learn from
that world, use the methods of its secular colleges, the
models of its business and management training
manuals, follow its one-man-ministry styles, copy its
music. We are even told we might call in and employ its
consultants who would help us to evaluate our assembly
programmes, reorganise our meetings, teach how to set
goals and reach them with set numbers in given periods.
Would God we had the courage to deal with these
intrusions as Nehemiah and his colleagues did.

2. A Change in Enemy Tactics

The swing from offers of help to anger and hostility
showed the true character of these would-be friends, and
this was to reveal itself in immediate and overt attack. First
they attempted to "weaken the hands" of the workers,
which probably means that, as the same enemies later did
when the wall was being built, they succeeded in
discouraging them by constant criticism and ridicule, a very
powerful weapon, especially when used against a people in
great weakness, poverty and even distress. The Israelites
had at that time no material defence and were probably
living in less than affluent conditions. An easy target for
cheap and callous mockery, they lost their zeal. It is not
hard to see a lesson from this for our own day.

Though weakened, the workers slowed the work, but did
not stop it. But the enemies would not be satisfied with less
than the abandoning the work. So, not content with insult
and slander, they now embarked on a campaign of false
accusation to the civil authorities by correspondence. Big
names are involved, titles are invoked. Artaxerxes the king,
Rehum the chancellor, Shimshai the scribe, and no less than
nine different nationalities (proving how right Nehemiah

was in excluding them from the work) as well as the great and noble Asnappar the king's predecessor. This unholy crew joined in accusing the Lord's people of rebellion, and the words fly: "wicked", "dishonour", "hurtful", "sedition", "they will impair the king's revenue", and shortly the king would have "no portion on this side of the river".

This is neither the first time nor the last that such tactics have been used against the Lord's people, from Daniel to Paul and onwards through the centuries, the prisons, the sword and fires of martyrdom have been used because of false accusations against Bible translators, preachers, and simple Christians as the Waldensians, Mennonites, Huguenots, Puritans, Presbyterians and many others. It is unlikely that it will disappear as a method of opposition. In this case it succeeded temporarily for we read the chilling words:

3. The work stopped

There is a strange and instructive angle to all this. In Ezra 5:6 we read that Tatnai the governor wrote to the capital to find out the truth of the whole matter and in due course Darius himself, having searched the archives found the orders of Cyrus and commanded that the Jews not only be left alone in their work but that they be supplied with money, materials, and even animals for sacrifice. Satan had overstepped himself, as he sometimes does, and good had come out of evil.

We must, however, realize that while at first glance it appears that it was the opposition which stopped the work, it is clear that this was not altogether the case. At the beginning of ch. 5 we read that when the work stopped the Lord sent two prophets, Haggai and Zechariah, who spoke to the people "in the name of the God of Israel". In the next verse we read that "then rose up Zerubbabel ... and Jeshua, and began to build the house of God which is at Jerusalem and with them were the prophets of God helping them."

It seems clear that the permission of Darius had not yet arrived and yet the building started, indicating that their own lack of dedication had been a great part of the problem. When we do not want to do something, it takes little to stop us. When we read the writings of the two prophets, we find no mention of the prohibition of the king nor the scheming of enemies, but we do find in the blunt and scathing messages of Haggai that they were excusing their lack of building the house of God by saying "the time is not yet". Meanwhile they were working away at the building and panelling of their own homes, and were engaged in business and money-making, even though the gains were insecure – the bags were full of holes.

Both Haggai and Zechariah also referred to defilement and uncleanness as being involved. Where there is sin, worldliness, greed, and laziness God's work has little chance, and we also can find reasons and excuses, many of them very real, though when we are in touch with God faith seeks ways around, through, or over the obstacles. It is also heart-warming to notice that the two prophets were more than preachers; they "were with the people ... helping them" in the work. Finally we read in 6:15 "This house was finished ... and the priests and the Levites with the rest of the children of the captivity kept the dedication of this house with joy".

4. Dedication of The Second Temple

The temple was neither an ornament nor yet a monument to the ardent nationalism or prowess of the Jews. It was, of course, a witness to the presence of God among His people, and was intended to be an expression of all that God was in the glory of holiness. But it was far more than this; it had another and prime purpose and that was to be a centre of the worship of the one and only true God. In this worship His people were also bearing witness to the fact that He was supreme in their lives no matter what gods others might follow. Since the church, both universal and local, is in the NT stated by God to be His temple or sanctuary in this age, all this should be true of every local church to-day. Read 1 Cor 3:16; Eph 2:21.

For this reason this temple of the restoration was dedicated or set apart publicly, consecrated to these purposes and no other. In earlier days the first temple had been dedicated as had the altar and all the furniture. God's house in those days must be seen by the whole world as something totally for God and therefore holy, and consecrated to Him and not to them or their use. It would also mean that this house would not be the result of copying the pagan temples around it, indeed its very difference would be part of its witness. We would venture to suggest that the same should be true of His house in this age also.

Once the house itself was in order there were sacrifices of dedication offered: bulls, rams and lambs, every one of which was a foreshadowing and a type of Christ in various aspects (Heb 9:9, 12-14). We notice that they offered twelve goats "as a sin offering for all Israel ... according to the twelve tribes of Israel". (It would seem that they knew nothing of the theory of "ten lost tribes"). The feasts of passover and unleavened bread were kept, as would be that of firstfruits so closely connected with them.

The end of ch. 6 tells us that they were able to do this, "for the priests and Levites had purified themselves together, all of them were pure (i.e. ritually pure) ... and the children of Israel which were come out of the captivity and all such as had separated themselves unto them from the filthiness of the heathen of the land ... did eat". These last were probably of the poorer folk who had not been taken to Babylon but who had corrupted themselves by settling into the ways of the pagans among whom they were living. What a joyful occasion as those representing "all Israel" gathered around the passover lamb with a purified priesthood and grateful hearts for all God's ways with them.

We cannot doubt the reality of this great revival, but

there were even greater things to come. God had given them leaders in Zerubbabel, Jeshua and others. In their weakness and defeat He had sent two great prophets, Haggai and Zechariah. He had given them for their worship purified priests, for without purity there can be no functioning priesthood and therefore no worship. There was however still much ignorance and confusion but God had a man in preparation who would fill that gap and bring them to the full joy of restoration and revival. His name was Ezra.

Chapter 19

Revival after the Exile:
The Second Stage

1. A Further Step Forward

THOUGH much had been achieved in clearing ground, building, dedication, renewing the feasts of Johovah, there was still much to be done. One great need was for teaching of the word of God, and the Lord was now about to supply that teaching through a specially prepared man and others who would join him in this important task. Special men seem to be provided by God in times of special need. Ezra was one such man, and though many others have appeared on the scene in all revivals this man was certainly of outstanding calibre.

There was much blessing and joy; much truth had been recovered in relation to the building and preparation of the temple with its feasts and offerings, but there had also appeared weakness, wavering, and backsliding as becomes clear from the reading the record of Haggai and Zechariah. The work had stopped altogether after the foundations were laid, an interruption which had its roots deep in their own lack of zeal for God's house while they themselves prospered and continued to see to their own ornate homes.

This had become so serious and so widespread that God had sent drought and famine to bring them to their senses (Hag 1:11). It is also evident from Hag 2 there there was a lack of purity of life among them (vv. 11-14). Where there is sin which is not dealt with, it is folly to expect true revival or blessing. For a clearer understanding of this both Haggai and Zechariah should be read, particularly Zech 1:4; 3:1-3; 5:1-3, with all three chapters of Haggai. The fact that God may in grace have given a measure of restoration does not justify complacency or lack of care. In fact alertness and humility are called for more than ever because Satan will use our carelessness as an opening for attack both from outside and inside. Teaching was urgently needed, and God had His man ready.

It is a sad truth, but a truth nonetheless, that revival, as we have said earlier, is not a one-act peak with a guaranteed continuance. It has to be maintained and renewed constantly or it may be lost. The revival had obviously lost its earlier drive and power. It was because of this that God brings on to the scene one of the most remarkable characters of the period and also of the Bible.

2. The Man Ezra
a. Earlier Preparation for Service

Ezra first appears in Ezra 7, and the question of exactly where he fits into the chronology of the period is not of special interest in these studies since we are seeking spiritual patterns which do not depend on chronological precision.

When he is first mentioned in our passage we are given the pedigree of Ezra right back to "Aaron the chief priest" showing that he was entitled to all the rights and privileges of priesthood. We are also told that he was ready, or skilled, in the law of Moses which the Lord God of Israel had given. Neither the priestly position which was his by birth, nor the authority which his commission from king Artaxerxes gave him, could make him a competent teacher of the sacred writings. Only diligent study could do that. Ironside speaks of "a competent, sober man of sound judgment, mighty in the Scriptures and an able instructor of his brethren; how invaluable he would be at this time".

His knowledge of the Holy Scriptures was also not merely intellectual, the result of scholastic training; the Spirit insists that already he "had prepared his heart to seek the law of the Lord." Paul prayed for the Ephesians (1:18) "that the eyes of your heart (JND & RV) might be enlightened, that you might know what is the hope of His calling." He first prepared his heart, not his head, and the reason for this is soon made clear for he sought the law of the Lord "that he might do it." The word of God would govern his affections and make him devoted totally to God; the teaching of others would follow. With him it was doing first and teaching afterwards. Like Jeremiah he could say "Thy words were found and I did eat them, and thy word was unto me the joy and rejoicing of my heart." Ezra was obviously not taking a course in Bible training to be a teacher, but he would practise it first and then be God's voice in leading His people back to Himself and on to closer obedience to all truth. It seems that once again we are being reminded that revival is a matter of heart and spirit, rather than of plans and programmes.

b. Links with the Past

This man's family-tree tells us more than that he was a descendant of Aaron, the first high priest of Israel. Though it does not contain every branch of that tree, it does mention that his great-grandfather was Hilkiah. We know from 2 Chron 34:14 that this Hilkiah was the priest who, in the days of king Josiah, had found in the rubble of the desecrated temple "the book of the law of the Lord". This discovery led to the last great revival before the deportation to Babylon. We have seen earlier that Zerubbabel who had a great part in this return from Babylon was the great-grandson of that same king Josiah. Again we have the thin red line of devoted souls passing on the truth of faithfulness to God in the darkest of days. We might wonder where Ezra, probably like Zerubbabel born in Babylon, would even find a copy of the Scriptures or go for help in their understanding, when he had "set his heart to seek the law of the Lord". The local Babylonian libraries and theological schools of that pagan land would be of no help. We do know, however, that there was at least one man who not only had a copy of the Scriptures but also studied them. That man was Daniel who was brought as a youth to

Babylon and, with three companions, was installed in the king's palace. He became a chief counsellor of that king, and remained to have the same office until the reign of Cyrus, the very one who had liberated all who wished to return to Jerusalem. Only in eternity shall we know what influence Daniel had on Cyrus in all of this.

Strangely there is nothing said of Daniel's family-tree except that he was of the tribe of Judah. Kings often in those days established captive princes in their palaces both as ornaments and, perhaps to keep a better eye on them, as hostages. It is possible that Daniel was of royal or at least noble blood, although this however is never mentioned in scripture. What is mentioned three times over is the fact that he was "greatly beloved", presumably by God (Dan 9:23; 10:11, 19).

In Dan 9:2 Daniel says that he "understood by [the] books the number of the years . . . [of] the desolations of Jerusalem". The only books containing such information would be the books of Scripture and he even tells us which of those books it was. An angel came to "give him understanding" of what he had read, for it could not be obtained in the schools of Babylon, and he who called him "greatly beloved" gives us at least part of the reason for this title. In Dan 10:12 he says "from the first day that thou didst set thine heart to understand and to chasten thyself before thy God, thy words were heard." We note the parallel between Daniel's "setting his heart to understand" and Ezra's "preparing his heart to seek the word of the Lord". Did the younger learn this secret from the older? It seems more than likely, indeed it has long been the writer's conviction that Daniel was the hinge in this whole story of the return, and what an important position that was! Daniel, so far as the record goes, was not privileged to return to Israel himself, probably because of his advanced age, or he may even have died by that time, but he had kept alive a fire that would break into flame and guide a whole new generation back to God and the truth of His house.

Chapter 20

Revival after the Exile: Restoration to the Land

1. The Journey from Babylon to Israel

IMMEDIATELY following the record of Ezra's preparation in diligent study of the Scripture and seeking God's will we have a record of the authority and instructions given him by the king. Six things stand out in these instructions (7:12-28).

1. In v. 12 the king, a pagan, recognises that Ezra is a scribe, or teacher, of the word or God. The idolatrous world knew the calibre of the man.

2. In v. 14 the king also acknowledges that everything in this venture must be done "according to the law of thy God which is thy hand". God seems to have made clear to Cyrus that all must be according to the book, since of himself and in his own cultural background there would be nothing to indicate such a thing.

3. The end of this verse shows clearly that Cyrus saw this land to be "in [Ezra's] hand." This would indicate that Ezra carried the book in his hand; before the king he was unashamedly and openly professed "a man of the book". A wonderful testimony before a pagan dictator!

4. In v. 25 there is a striking statement which must have been put in the king's heart by God whether he understood it or not. Ezra is charged that any man in the new community at Jerusalem whom he, Ezra, might put in any place of authority or leadership must be one "who knows the law of the Lord thy God." Would to God that we had always been careful about this, for we have erred greatly in allowing men to occupy places of rule or oversight in the assembly who, in spite of the clear

132

teaching of 1 Tim 3 and Titus 1 are deficient in the qualities required of an elder. And we have reaped a sad harvest as a result. It is not enough that a man may be successful in business, a good organiser, well-educated secularly or theologically, strong in personality, or eloquent. By the same token it is not enough that he be old, or even older, or that he simply may have been there "from the beginning". He simply *must* be one well grunded in "the laws of his God".

5. In the same v. 25 Ezra is told that if there is a lack of such men he is not to accept a lower standard, but rather that he "teach them that know not".

6. All to be done was to be "according to the wisdom of thy God which is in thy hand".

It is no wonder that in view of this Ezra bursts out in v. 27 in an exclamation of worship: "Blessed be the Lord God of our fathers who has put such a thing as this in the king's heart." None of this goes to the head of this man of God, nor does he even allow us to think that it happened because of any ability on his part. His humble cry is "[God] hath extended mercy unto me before the king . . . and I was strengthened as the hand of the Lord my God was upon me."

2. A Survey of Conditions

Ezra apparently at this point started on the four month journey to Israel, but before he did so we are given a careful listing of the names of the "chief of their fathers, and the genealogies of them that went up . . ." (8:1). We note first that God knew by name all who were willing to get out of Babylon and move to Canaan to work for Him, whatever branch of work they might be engaged in. No worker need ever imagine that he is forgotten or that his person or work is unnoticed or unimportant. All who obeyed were recorded by name as under His eye and care at all times. This is not less but rather more apparent in the NT where the very hairs of their head are numbered. How grateful we should be that it is so, especially when we are so little in the estimation of the world and sometimes may ·be¡ even forgotten by our fellow Christians.

Before they went far Ezra called a halt, made a camp, "viewed the people", and found deficiencies. There were no Levites, and this was a very serious matter. These were the servants of the house of the Lord who had carried the tabernacle through the wilderness, acting not only as its bearers but also erecting and dismantling it at every camping place throughout the forty years. They also were its designated guardians and protectors who had to pitch their tents immediately around its three closed sides while Moses, Aaron and his sons (also of course of the tribe of Levi) had their tents before the gate of the court. Levites also had charge of looking after the materials of the offerings and were servants to assist the priests in their work. They were also the teachers of the people (Num 3, 4; Deut 33:8-10; 2 Chron 17:8, 9). At Sinai they numbered 8,580, and in the many years in the land they must have increased greatly in numbers as did all the tribes.

In the movement we are studying the Levites appear to have been lacking in commitment to God. In the first company to come to Israel with Zerubbabel, there were one hundred and twenty eight singers, but only seventy-four Levites (Ezra 2:40, 41). Now in Ezra's there were none at all. It would seem that it has always been easier to find more singers than servants.

Servants in the house of God were very important in those days and are even more so to-day, yet it always seems hard to find such. The model, of course, is our Lord who said: "I am among you as one who serves". He also said "He that would be great among you shall be servant of all". The apostle Paul, who signed himself "servant (bondservant) of

Jesus Christ" also wrote in 2 Cor 4:5: "We preach not ourselves but Christ Jesus the Lord, and ourselves your servants for Jesus' sake". One of our most urgent needs today is for servants for the house of the Lord, Levites who carry, serve, guard, and teach, and such are absolutely vital if we are to have revival, or even survival. Yet the cry seems to be for "leadership", or training for it, or finding out whether or not we have leadership qualities. Like the disciples around the supper table in John 13, no one is willing to be a servant – except the Lord. Indeed we learn from the parallel passage in Luke that on the way there they had been disputing about who would be greatest in the kingdom.

That Ezra called a halt at the beginning of his trip in order to review the people marks him as a prudent leader who believed in surveying the whole situation, finding out who was with him and who was not. Our Lord gave some very specific instruction on this when he said that a man who was faced with attack by an enemy should "sit down" and count the cost. This is exactly what Ezra did, and he not only discovered a serious weakness; he refused to proceed until it was remedied. Sometimes we think we can improvise and things will work themselves out as we go along. This is always a delusion, and Ezra was aware of the danger involved in such thinking. He was not only a man of perception, but also a man of action.

He called nine men who were "chief men", probably chiefs or elders of clans, and two others who are simply called "men of understanding". Happy are those who have such men of prestige, moral authority, and experience as the first group, but what an extra blessing are men of understanding. The fact that understanding is mentioned along with knowledge and wisdom several times in the OT makes it clear that it is to be distinguished from them, and is more than either. Knowledge we may gather from a variety of sources and in many ways. Wisdom is the ability to apply such knowledge, for it is possible to have all kinds of knowledge and yet not be wise. Understanding seems to be the ability not merely to know and to be able to act on our knowledge but to see below the surface and be able to grasp what it all means – to grasp the principles and purposes involved. It means much more than cleverness or smartness of which we have an abundant supply everywhere, and some astonishing demonstrations of its use. The heart cry of God Himself through Moses in Deut 32:29 is; "Oh that they were wise, that they understood this". Understanding the ways of God would lead them to look further down the road, and consider long-term consequences rather than seeing only the short-term statistics.

These men were sent back with orders to find and bring "servants for the house of our God", and they succeeded in finding another man of understanding who brought with him thirty-eight Levites, a shockingly small number. They also came however with two hundred and twenty Nethinim, who, though not Levites by birth, or even Israelites, had been inducted into some level of service for the Levites, having been given for this by "David and the princes". The Jewish historian Josephus refers to them as "temple slaves" in his time. It is interesting that they are mentioned by this name only in these books of Ezra and Nehemiah, and once again, in 1 Chron 9:2. Whoever and whatever they were it was a sad day when the real Levites were so selfish and and uncaring that they did not respond to the challenge, so that others not indicated for the job should have to do it. This must have been a burden to Ezra as we gather from the following verses. The bringing in of Nethinim in place of Levites must also have been a rebuke for the Levites. It does remind us of a Biblical principle that, if the desired instrument or vessel is not available, God may be forced to pass on to some other instrument, the latter taking the crown of the former (Rev 3:11; Esther 4:14).

The shaken and grieved leader remained at the river Ahava announcing a general fast that they "might afflict themselves before God, to seek of Him a right way for us and for our little ones, and for all our substance" – a lesson for us on the place of prayer in times of disappointment.

According to v. 23 God heard them and, assured of their way, they set off. Then, significantly, all the precious things they were carrying back for the temple were carefully weighed and distributed among those entrusted with their safe-keeping while the following solemn charge was laid on them: "Ye are holy unto the Lord; the vessels are holy also . . . watch ye, and keep them until ye weigh them before the chief of the priests . . . at Jerusalem, in the chambers of the house of the Lord". On arrival in the holy land, each man gave account of his faithful guardianship of the holy things. What a lesson we may learn from this, for we too are carrying across the wilderness of the present age the holy things of the Lord, knowing that "we shall all stand before the judgment seat of Christ" and that "every man shall give account of himself to God" (Rom 14:10, 12). It is in light of this that Paul entreated: "O Timothy, keep that which is committed to thy trust" (1 Tim 6:20; 2 Tim 1:12, 14).

Chapter 21

Revival after the Exile: Problems in the Land

1. The Imperative of Separation

MAKING a start was good, as was the halt to correct deficiencies and grieve with fasting and prayer over such. Finishing the journey to the land was also a laudable accomplishment, and so too was the safe arrival of all the valuables for which each bearer had been made accountable. It soon became clear, however, that with all this done there would be other trying confrontations and much with which to deal before Israel could push forward with the spiritual movement.

No sooner had they reached the land than further problems met them, for Satan will never give up trying to thwart any work that is of God. He knew that one of the quickest ways of destroying this movement would be to corrupt the people. They had sadly failed in maintaining godly separation from the world around them. They knew the truth of this separation quite clearly, but knowing the truth and practising it are not the same thing. No further back in this very book of Ezra than 6:21 we read that only those who had separated themselves from the filthiness of the Gentiles of the land could gather to keep the passover.

Not only the word "separation" but the very concept is often treated in our day with carelessness, disdain, or mockery; it is seen as the badge of narrow-mindedness and bigotry. Some of this has been provoked no doubt by the misuse of the word to excuse carnal and wrongheaded divisions which have been caused in many instances not by legitimate spiritual concern, but by personality clashes, wrangling over unimportant details, or even misguided stubbornness. Having said this, and said it with deep sorrow and regret, separation from the world, from "the unclean thing", from all teaching false to the fundamentals of Holy Scripture remains a basic Biblical doctrine, whether we like it or not.

The Biblical doctrine of separation

Because Abraham had been called out of Babylon to father a new nation he must "walk before God and be perfect." Isaac must not have a bride from the idolatrous nations around him. Intermarrying was prohibited since it would lead to corruption and ruination.

In Num 25 twenty-four thousand died because they joined in the religious festivities of the Moabites at Baal-Peor which led to adultery and in some cases intermarriage. The story is so important that it is referred to in Nehemiah, Micah, 2 Peter, Jude, and Revelation.

In Josh 23:12 the prohibition is repeated and the reasons for it given to the new generation now entering the promised land. Later on Solomon's sin in this matter led to the great division of the nation, generations of all sorts of trouble and the final judgment of God.

In the NT the doctrine of separation is no less clear. The prayer of our Lord for His own whom the Father had "given [Him] out of the world" was "They are not of the world, sanctify (or separate) them through thy truth."

In Eph 5:11 after mentioning some of the sins of the age we read "be not ye partakers with them ... have no fellowship with the unfruitful works of darkness."

In James 1:27 the beliver must "keep himself unspotted from the world."

There is much more in a similar vein but this should suffice for our study.

The Seriousness of Disobedience

It is important to understand the seriousness of the

situation which Ezra faced in chs. 9 and 10 of his book before he even started his very important part in the revival. He knew, and we should know, that there can be no true and completed revival until such situations are dealt with and put right. His personal reaction, especially when told that the princes and rulers were the chief culprits, was to tear his clothes in grief, not halting at putting ashes on his head in mourning but tearing his hair out; he "sat down astonished", or as in some translations – dumbfounded. It is comforting to see that in the following verse we read that everyone who trembled at the words of the God of Israel rallied to him and they sat in shame until the hour of the evening sacrifice. Note that it was trembling in awe and fear at God's Word which characterised this group. One fears we have drifted far from this attitude of reverence and fear before the word of God.

In his desperation Ezra did not do what many would have been tempted to do: go to the people and try to talk to them. This would come later, but the first thing is to fall on his knees before God and cry out "Oh my God, I am ashamed and blush to lift up my face to thee for *our* iniquities are increased over our heads . . ."

The similarity between this and Daniel's confession is striking. Whatever else Daniel may have achieved in those dark seventy years, to have been the mentor and model for a deliverer like Ezra was well worth the price. Compare Ezra with Dan 9.

2. Prayer and Confession

Joshua, devastated by the defeat before Ai, went in and lay on his face before God. God, however, had to remind him after a while, that it was no longer a time for prayer but for action: judging the sin and bringing the people back to obedience in the fear of God. Ezra did not need God to remind him, for during his time of prayer in the open "before the house of God, a very great congregation of men, and women, and children had gathered to him: for the people wept very sore". God and His servant Ezra are dealing with sin and with hearts, not with numbers, goals, and human plans. These men knew better; indeed it would have seemed strange to them to seek help in the affairs of God's house from God's enemies.

In a flash the challenge is handed to him by the concerned ones among the Lord's people: "Arise, for this matter belongeth to thee; we also will be with thee: be of good courage and do it. Then arose Ezra . . ." No time was lost since there was concern for the wrong that had been done to God. One would wish that elders and leaders in our day were concerned enough to get up and act as this man did. No there was no shilly-shallying, no politicking nor seeking a consensus as politicians do in governmental affairs since they are dependent on votes to retain their positions. There is no trying to find out if the move will be acceptable or popular, or even look for a preacher to consult, or how many dissenters there may be. His anguish over sin has hown the people how terrible it was, and they are all there weeping, and weeping together without dividing into men's, women's and young people's groups.

It was a time of cold and rain in which the people shivered (10-9), and Ezra had had no food (v. 6). But nothing must hinder this work of dealing with sin, so in v. 14 the leaders were challenged first for they had sinned. They were called upon to "stand and with them the elders" and those who were guilty must act immediately. In v. 18 we see that some of the priests were guilty, even the sons of the high priest.

It is just possible that some sort of extenuating circumstance could have been pleaded, perhaps that not as many women had accompanied the men from Babylon. It was not a day for excuses. What was wrong must be put right if they were to go on in this great revival. We could learn from them at every step, especially in the matter of worldly entanglements.

Chapter 22

Revival after the Exile: The Great National Bible Reading

Expounding the Scripture

IN the previous chapter Ezra certainly acted with courage and vigour. He knew that all activity, however good and well-intentioned, would be a waste of time if obvious and acknowledged sin were not dealt with. Now that this had been done there was a felt and understood need for positive instruction. The initiative for this came in a very spontaneous way from the people themselves. The cry went up to "Bring the book" and "all the people" gathered themselves together in the main square of the city.

Surely this was one of the most impressive gatherings of the whole Bible. In our last chapter we read of a gathering in Ezra 10 but, whatever way we look at the chronology of these books, it cannot be the same as the one we are about to consider. The previous one was pinpointed as on the twentieth day of the ninth month, while this one was "when the seventh month had come"; it was probably held at the beginning of it. The previous one began with Ezra in prayer and confession, then calling the people together and demanding in the name of God that they be done with the illegal entanglements with the pagan world around them. There is no record of a great Bible exposition such as we have here, and surely this must be a model for all would-be expositors and teachers of God's word.

a. Opposition to Building the Wall

Before dealing with Ezra, his great Bible study and its results, we must take a look at what had happened between the last gathering we considered in Ezra 10 and this one in

Neh 8. The time between had been difficult and discouraging. The wall had been completed or nearly so. There had been a change in the tactics of the enemies who (alas) had apparently wormed their way into the hidden fabric of the community. The leaders of this campaign of opposition appear in one grouping or another in six passages in the book of Nehemiah, five of them in connection with the building of the wall of Jerusalem, an operation which obviously stirred their anger. In the book of Ezra we have already found a strong opposition group working against the building of the temple and, at one point, bringing the work to a halt. A few names of leaders are given in that story but we do not hear of them again. Now, as a start was made on the wall, a new group appears to do what they can to hinder and disturb.

These walls were necessary in that turbulent period, especially for a small and resented people recently returned from captivity. They were trying to build for God in a land into which others had come making false claims of ownership (an exact picture of our position in relation to the god and prince of this present scene). It is not that everyone would live, or even want to live, within these city walls. We are told in fact, in 7:73 that "the priests, the Levites, the porters, the singers and all Israel dwelt in their (own) cities". The wall of Jerusalem, as in all cities of antiquity, was for the defence of the temple, the government, and those functioning in these at their appointed periods of service (see Luke 1:8-9). In time of war it was also at least temporary shelter to which people from the surrounding country could flee. It is hard to understand why some of their neighbours became so agitated about this simple defence against intruders which could never by any stretch of imagination be seen as a threat against anyone. It was for defence only.

It might help us to understand if we were to look at a parallel phenomenon in our own day. We observe a hard-to-understand hostility towards any kind of spiritual defence in a local congregation of Christians. The almost paranoic preoccupation with openness is so general in some quarters that even sincere Christians who should know better become either apologetic about it or else join the chorus that in the church there is no such thing as a wall of any kind. With respect, we would venture to register our dissent.

It may be true that in the NT there is no mention of walls as such; indeed it is often pointed out that in John 10, while Israel is referred to as a fold, the "other sheep" of this age are referred to as a flock. This is pointed out with remarks which might be paraphrased as "See! There are no walls or fences in the church." We must all be glad that in one sense the local church is not, or at least should not be, an isolated garrison with locked gates and a moat and wall bristling with all sorts of mechanisms to keep everybody out who is not in possession of some sacred shibboleth or password. There may indeed be some places like this and we have little sympathy with their attitude. We have, however, just as little sympathy with those who see a local assembly of believers as a sort of public park into which, or through which, anyone may stroll at will with no thought of any responsibility in it or acceptance of its beliefs, concerns, doctrines, or disciplines, or of subjection to these. This kind of assembly or church is also seen as an ecclesiastical cafeteria where they can take what they want, and reject what is not to their taste, a restaurant which they may leave for another more to their liking, where "their needs will be better met" and to which they may return with no questions asked if it suits them to do so. This sort of thing bears little resemblance to a NT local church, at least as we see it.

b. Safeguards and Defences in the New Testament Church

In a NT church, while there were no man-made or artificial barriers to keep genuine and sincere Christians out, there was obviously spiritual care taken that none but true believers were admitted or welcomed to its fellowship. In Acts 9:26 when Saul of Tarsus came to Jerusalem after his conversion, news of which had apparently not yet reached that city, he attempted to join himself to the company of Christians there. They were unwilling to accept him until Barnabas introduced him as a believer, upon which he was gladly received into the fellowship. That very simple and uncontrived story shows clearly that these earliest Christians did not leave it up to the individual whether or not he should come in to participate in the Lord's supper and share in the local fellowship. We see this as a defence against the intrusion of those who have no right to such a place.

In Acts 5:11-14 we read that after the disciplining of Ananias and Sapphira; "great fear came upon all the church . . . and they were all with one accord together in Solomon's porch, and of the rest durst no man add himself to them." This may mean that the holiness of God as reproduced and exhibited in the church was so rearl and visible, as also was God's judgment on anything compromising that holiness, that it kept the unconverted or any spurious adherents from attempting to join the company. It may also mean, though less probably, that it had been made very clear that only the sincere and genuine would be welcome. Whichever view we take, it is evident that there was a very effective defence in the early church against false professors finding their way in among the believers. The spiritual perception of Peter in seeing through the unreality of Simon the sorcerer in Acts 8:20 is evidence of the same kind of thing. Peter's handling of it is sharp and to the point: "Thou hast neither part nor lot in this matter; for thy heart is not right in the sight of God".

This is far from the decision of Luther and most of his fellow reformers, who decided that to restrict church membership to those who proved themselves to be genuine believers would reduce their effectiveness because of smallness of numbers. Menno Simons, after whom the

Mennonites were nicknamed, took an opposite view, and for his pains he and his followers were ruthlessly persecuted and some of them martyred. It is interesting to note the full cycle through which we seem to have come historically in this reasoning. Surely we do not need to make it clear that we are not even thinking of people, Christian or non-Christian, who may come into or attend our public services as visitors, to whom we should extend a warm welcome.

In 1 Cor 5:12 the Holy Spirit through Paul emphasises the fact that there *is* an inside and an outside to the local church, and that while the church has nothing to do with trying to rule or discipline those "outside" they are held responsible by God for those who are "inside". They must "put away from among themselves" the person living in sin. They were to acknowledge the divinely-instituted demarcation to which Paul drew attention.

In Acts 6 disputes among Christians were to be settled *within* the local fellowship and the taking of them to outside arbitration was strictly forbidden. Read also 1 Cor 6.

In 1 Tim 1:19-20 the Holy Spirit in a letter instructing Timothy "how one ought to behave oneself *in* the household of God which is the church of the living God", tells of some who had "made shipwreck concerning the faith"; already they had been "delivered to Satan, that they may learn not to blaspheme". They failed to recognise the sanctity *within* the local assembly.

We suggest that these and other Scriptures indicate that the primitive church was well supplied with defences against all sorts of threatening intrusions; these would answer to the walls of Jerusalem at which we have been looking in Nehemiah. We believe that these defences are important and that we remove or neglect them at our own peril, however loud the clamour might be for such a move, on the grounds that it is more "progressive".

Chapter 23

Revival after the Exile: Nehemiah's Opponents

1. Foreign adversaries

THE first notice of these enemies is in Neh 2:10 where we read that they "were grieved that there was come a man to seek the welfare of the children of Israel". There are two mentioned: Sanballat the Horonite (which labels him as being from Moab) and Tobiah the servant, an Ammonite. This pair had a bad pedigree for we learn from Gen 19 that these two races sprang from the drunken incest of Lot with his two daughters. Their nations' territory was on the east side of Jordan but they had obviously infiltrated the patrimony of Israel, so we do not wonder that they were grieved. Any man caring for the welfare of Israel was their greatest dread, obviously he who would stir their bitter animosity.

Joined by a third member called Geshem the Arab, who is referred to in other places as Gashmu, they make their first move quickly (2:19). Their first round is one of mockery, and this has ever been a ready weapon of those who wish to attack. In ch.4 they move from scorn and ridicule to anger and great indignation, and they now use the 'threat of an "army of Samaria". The next step in opposition is in vv. 7, 8 where these men, joined by Arabs, Ammonites, and Ashdodites (Philistines), form a conspiracy "to come and fight against Jerusalem and to hinder it". To all of these tactics God's people replied by praying.

In ch. 6 they changed the attack and now suggested a conference or summit meeting on the plain, to which Nehemiah gave his classic and oft-quoted reply: "I am doing a great work and therefore I cannot come down". To

147

leave the heights of Jerusalem and come down to their level of debate would not only have been a waste of time but also highly dangerous.

The saddest and most dangerous development is recorded in 6:17-19 where we read of a clandestine operation by infiltrating the ranks of the faithful with smooth words and promises which won over even some of the nobles of Judah who entered into negotiations, and pledged themselves to the enemy. Did these nobles of Judah think for a moment that if such tricksters as these from Moab, Ammon, Arabia, and Ashdod had their way there would be any real future for the nobles of Judah? One is amazed at the gullibility of these men, but it is a ploy which has worked often and is still working. It was this, of course, which led to intermarriages, a situation which culminated in the son of the high priest marrying the daughter of Tobias and moving him into an apartment in the temple itself! This was the Trojan horse tactic with a vengeance! Another of the high priest's family married a daughter of Sanballat, perhaps to keep up with the movement and prove himself unbigoted and progressive. (Read Neh 13:28.)

2. The Set Feasts

The seventh month in the sacred calendar of Israel had special significance for it marked the beginning of the last group of set seasonal feasts of Jehovah to which we have referred earlier. In this month came the feasts of trumpets (or gathering), atonement, and tabernacles. These were held in the end of the harvest of fruit, oil, and wine; they closed the Jewish cycle of holy feasts, and foreshadowed prophetically the rounding off of Israel's national history in regathering, atonement, and the sabbatical Messianic kingdom. But for this remnant regathered to Jerusalem, it had a present and very real meaning.

There were the already noted signs of failure and deterioration in the revival. These had left scars and also unhealed wounds of which the people seem to have become conscious. At such a time, and with such a spiritual need they gathered to their ancient and holy city and unanimously cried, "Bring the book!" The people knew whom to call when they wanted to hear from "the book", for he was the man who, long before, had prepared his heart to study the book.

Would to God that this cry were oftener heard among us – "Bring the book". There is a growing weariness with oft-peddled little sermons, however well prepared and honed, with the "how-to" books, the endless "counselling" and "consulting" prescriptions and recipes with their liberal sprinkling of the "in" terminology of the intellectual, theological, and business spheres. There is a growing hunger for the more substantial and satisfying exposition of Holy Scripture which is not only upbuilding but corrective and restorative. Perhaps this is where we should start in our praying for revival – "Bring the book!" Let us get back to the Word, but with humbled hearts and seeking to learn of God and what He wants us to be and do, rather than to parade our learning or provide quick and painless cures for our problems.

3. Bring the Book!

The Bible is a book of drama, and where would we find a more dramatic scene than that of Neh 8? On a raised scaffolding of some sort stands what some would consider an obscure little man holding a book or scroll. He has no impressive title; nor is he of royal stock. He was born in Babylon during the captivity and therefore was not likely to have been a product of the theological schools. His name is said to mean "help". Although of the priestly family, another was high priest and he is never referred to as having any special priestly position. He is called a Levite; they were "the servants of the house of the Lord". The only claim made for him is that "he was a ready scribe in the law

of the Lord"; we would say he was competent in the
Scriptures.

He had disappeared from the narrative of the two books
we have been considering and we are not sure where he
was, or even if he had been in the land at all, since several
of these men had to go back and forth between the two
communities, one in Israel, the other in Babylon. He does
not appear to have had any fixed responsibility either in a
school or congregation and would therefore be classified as
a mere itinerant Bible teacher. His prestige was spiritual,
and the call of the people was not for Ezra as a man, but for
the book of which he was the custodian, the student, and
the champion.

We are impressed immediately by the words that follow,
for we read that before the congregation Ezra brought the
law, and that is the word of God. He did not bring his
ideas, plans, or philosophies to this hungry, yearning
people; he was not interested in entertaining them, or in
getting them emotionally stirred up to commit themselves
to goals for growth. He confronted them with the claims of
God as found in His word, and that word did its own work in
their hearts and consciences.

We note also that he did not feel any need to divide the
people of God into groups, either by sex or age. "Men,
women, and all who could hear with understanding" were
there, for they had not been hypnotised by the educational
theories of the Prof. Deweys of their day, so they did not
feel it was necessary to send their children to the basement
to be entertained or play games while the parents heard the
word of God explained. It was the feast of trumpets so all
work was suspended while they gathered to Jerusalem, for
this people did not take advantage of the holiday to go for a
trip with the family. They brought the family with them to
hear the Scriptures, all of them together, men, women, and
all who could understand; this is repeated in the passage for
emphasis that we might not miss the point.

The Scriptures were read to them from morning until midday. In our day people can easily stand for this length of time watching sports events, movies, or concerts, but not more than an hour over the Word. Even when gathered to hear the Word, the arrangements must be for an order more and more like the programmes of those around us. These people were in earnest, so frills and entertainments were of no interest to them. They were conscious of a deep spiritual need and realised that such need could only be met from the book.

In contrast with the above we quote from a recent book by a certain doctor (presumably of theology) who calls himself "a catalyst for growth and renewal." He makes the following suggestions for improving our meetings and attracting more people: "special musical numbers, interviews, singing, drama, five-minute slide shows, poems, monologues and a maximum twenty-five-minute message" – all packed into one hour!

Chapter 24

Revival after the Exile: The Word Acknowledged

1. Attitude and Response to the Word of God

THE attitude of any Christian to God's word and his consequent response to it is vitally important, and God has recorded a pattern for us in Neh 8:1-12.

1. There was a *determination* to have the Word and nothing else; "Bring the book" was the heart-cry of a whole people.
2. The word's *importance* was such that they were happy to give it time "from early morning until midday".
3. Their whole and earnest *attention* was given to it and no distractions were allowed. "The ears of all the people were attentive to the book." The same word for "attentive" here is used by Nehemiah in Neh 1:6 when he wanted the full attention of God to his prayer; the same root is in Ps 130: "Lord, hear my voice: let thine ears be attentive to the voice of my supplications". The whole and undivided attention of eyes and ears requested by the prophet and the psalmist to their cry of agony and distress is the kind of attention given to God and His word by this people who want nothing less than a reply from God through His word.
4. There is an expressed *reverence* for the Word for we read that when the book was opened before them "all the people stood up". What a moment of high drama this must have been for the servant of God! And how stimulating and rewarding to him! We see little of this in our day, when our jaded tastes have to be catered to.
5. There was heart *assent* to what was read, and *acceptance*

of its message in the words "Amen! Amen!" which mean "Let it be so", or "Let it be done".

6. There was *submission* to the word, indicated by the "bowing of their heads."

7. There was *worship* of the Lord with their faces to the ground. They gave God his true place of worth, this thought being inherent in our word "worship-worthship."

8. There was *weeping* in conviction, repentance, and sorrow for sin (v.9), while in v.17 "there was very great *gladness*" as they took the very first step in obedience in keeping the feast of booths or tabernacles.

This is more than a pattern of revival; it is the very core and essence of it, and we believe there are no shortcuts.

Chapter 25

Revival after the Exile: The Model Messenger

1. The Leadership

SINCE in these studies we are searching for "patterns" we do well to pay attention to Neh 8:7, 8 and the pattern of message which achieved results. Ezra was not alone in what was going on and in this he was a wise leader. In v.7 we read the names of thirteen men who shared in the teaching, as well as "the Levites", and in v.9 we learn that Nehemiah, though he was Tirshatha or Governor, was also with Ezra in this work. The man who imagines that he can go in and lead a revival or renewal is either extremely arrogant or extremely foolish.

There was a great flaw in the work and career of Samson who was intended by God to be the deliverer of His people, and who actually "began" to be moved by the Spirit of the Lord (Judges 13:25). He did some very spectacular things including the slaying of one thousand Philistines with the jaw-bone of a donkey, killing thirty men at his own wedding party, killing a lion, breaking heavy cables with which he had been bound, carrying the great gates of a city away on his back, pulling an entire building down on top of himself and everybody else, thus killing more people in his death than he did in all his life. The flaw was that while he did all these things on his own, he never once, so far as the record goes, associated the people with him in his battles. In this he differed from Othniel, Gideon, Jephtha and indeed most of the other judges. When he died so spectacularly he left Israel still under the yoke of the Philistines. There must be a lesson for us in his history.

2. Their Public Readings

Of the ministry of all these men and Ezra we read that "they read in the book in the law of God distinctly, and gave the sense, and caused them to understand the reading". In this we have the three pillars of all truly expository teaching, and surely all teaching from God's word has to be expository, else it would be the intrusion of our ideas where they never should be found. The three pillars are:

1. They read in the book of the law of God *distinctly*. This word, only this once so translated, seems to have the meaning of doing it in such a way that it will be clear and understandable. We recommend this to all who would read God's word publicly. It should be read reverently, clearly, distinctly (as opposed to mumbling), carefully but with intonation and proper emphasis, and above all with feeling. To do this may mean that we read it to ourselves before we try to do so publicly, that we assure ourselves that we have grasped its meaning, that we make sure we have the correct pronunciation of the words before we start. It is God's word and deserves to be read accurately and intelligently, indeed if it is to do its job it *must be so read*.

2. They gave *the sense*. The Scriptures they were reading were written in the ancient or classical Hebrew, but they had been speaking Aramaic for seventy years in Babylon so probably many of the less-educated classes born in captivity would not be fluent in Hebrew. It was therefore necessary to explain what the actual text meant. This is true exposition.

3. They caused the people to *understand*, which would refer to the applicaation of the message, bringing them under its power and demanding a response to its demands.

We recommend this pattern for all worthwhile teaching of God's word as being just as valid and as necessary to-day as in Ezra's day. Teaching recorded for us in the Scriptures seems never to have been given merely for information, much less for ostentation, but always to be acted upon and lived by. It always demanded a response, whether in the teaching of Christ Himself or any other servant of God. The expressions: "Go and do thou likewise", "If ye know these things, happy are ye if ye do them", "He that heareth ... and doeth ... is a wise man ...", "I wrote to see whether ye would obey", "If ye then be risen with Christ, seek ... set your affection ... mortify ... put off ... put on ... lie not ..." (Col 3), "I delivered you ... I gave you a land ... therefore ... choose ye this day" (Josh 24), "I have set before you ... therefore choose" (Deut 30:19) and so on everywhere. Teaching, when accepted and responded to must produce some sort of result. It is never an end in itself.

Most of what follows in this great revival has been discussed in the previous studies, and therefore needs little more comment. Having pledged themselves to obedience to God's word the rest was merely a question of finding out what that word required and doing it without delay or question. They separated themselves from everything displeasing to God; they kept the feasts, however irrelevant some of them, such as tabernacles, might have seemed; they reinstated the various functions of priests and Levites and poured out generously for the support of all services and sacrifices. They corrected a number of abuses and exploitations, put right much which had been wrong. The end result in every case was great joy and blessing, and all sprang from total obedience to the word of the Lord.

It is the thesis of this study that we do have patterns of revival carefully recorded for us by God Himself. Since they are divine patterns we believe that we can neither add to them nor substitute for them schemes of our own. We also believe that to ignore them is to shut the door on all hopes of genuine spiritual revival.

Chapter 26

An Abortive Revival Under Asa

1 Kings 15:9 to 16:14 and 2 Chron 14:1 to 16:13

1. Early Promise

WE have studied the positive side of revival and the patterns they give us in the days of Joshua, Samuel, Hezekiah, Josiah, and Ezra/Nehemiah. In our introduction other cases were cited where revivals, begun apparently with very good intentions, for various reasons failed and left the nation to revert to its previous condition. Much can be learned by noting the reasons for the failures just as we have learned from the successes.

King Asa was the grandson of Rehoboam whose folly and disobedience had precipitatd the division of the nation into north and south, Israel and Judah. Grandson of Solomon, he was also related to David through Absalom as his mother Maacha was granddaughter of that rebel prince. Asa started well having obviously seen the fruits of the sad departure in the days of his father and more particularly of his grandfather under whom idolatry flourished in all its basest and most depraved forms. Even sodomy became rampant, probably as part of the worship of the Asherah (1 Kings 14:22-24). Asa began by removing and destroying the idols, their altars, the high places, and the groves (Asherah). God blessed him in this and gave him rest through these years, so he built or restored fortress cities, seeing the importance of defending Judah against the inroads of corruption. Thus he demonstrated that he knew how to build up as well as how to tear down, a good balance.

At this point he was tested by a very serious invasion by Zerah king of Ethiopia with an army of one million, and three hundred chariots. Some believe that at this time Zerah ruled over Egypt, Israel's relentless enemy. Asa knew that he was no match for such a foe. His short but wonderful prayer of total dependence on God and absolute faith in Him is found in 2 Chron 14:11; it is a model in itself. God answered, and smote the Ethiopians who were overthrown and driven away as far as Gerar in the extreme south-west borders in Philistia; all of that country was looted by Judah, probably for having joined Zerah in the invasion.

On his return to Jerusalem the king was met by the prophet Azariah with a message of strength and encouragement as well as a warning. Among other things the message said: "The Lord is with you while you be with Him; but if you forsake Him He will forsake you ... Be strong therefore and let not your hands be weak, for your work shall be rewarded". These words, we are told, made the king "take courage". "And he put away the abominable idols ... and renewed the altar of the Lord that was before the porch of the Lord." He then had the joy of seeing many from the northern kingdom joining him at Jerusalem where they offered sacrifices to God. He went on to take what was no doubt one of the hardest steps of all by removing his mother from her position as queen because she had made an idol ("horrible thing") in a grove. The idol he cut down, shattered and burnt in the brook Kidron. Like Gideon he had to face his stiffest job in breaking family idols, but he triumphed in it. All this was most commendable, and he apparently meant business for he went further and restored to the temple all the things which he and his father had dedicated for this purpose (1 Kings 15:15).

We do read in 2 Chron 15:17 that "the high places were not taken away" which may refer not to the high places of the idols but to the fact that the people, as in other times, offered sacrifices to God on high places rather than in Jerusalem, something prohibited by God. The fact that in the verse it says "nevertheless the heart of Asa was perfect all his days" probably means that his intentions were sincere but the people were simply not ready to follow his lead in this matter. This lack of a broad-based teaching of the people was a danger which Asa's son who succeeded him tried to remedy (2 Chron 17: 8, 9). In all of this one rejoices, feeling that a lasting revival was on the way, and all of it is certainly to be commended.

There was also peace in the land from his fifteenth year until his thirty-fifth, when there came a disastrous stumble which set everything back. He was then a relatively old man with only five more years of his life left, and it seems such a pity that his revival collapsed after having achieved so much.

2. A Great Mistake

2 Chronicles 16: 1-6

In looking for patterns and principles we have already seen in almost every revival that when a work is being done for God, Satan will always attack, and though his tactics vary, his purpose is always the same.

Baasha king of the breakaway northern kingdom of Israel, after years without a major war, suddenly "came up against Judah, and built Ramah", presumably so that he could cut off the route of those who were leaving his country to return to the land and worship of their fathers in Jerusalem. It was to be a sort of Berlin Wall between north and south. Ramah is a mere six miles or so north-west of Jerusalem and the "building" of it probably means turning it into a fortress or defence city. It would have been a serious threat to Judah since it could be used as a spearhead aimed at the capital. There is no doubt at all as to the seriousness of this threat and Asa was justified in feeling the need for action. It is at this point that we are shocked at the action he took. He chose to use the world's tactics in the things of God. He would do what statesmen and politicians have done all through the ages down to our own days; to distract an enemy and thwart his attack by getting a third party to attack him from behind. It was a standard human ploy, but there were a number of things wrong with it in this case.

Firstly, this man's father had completely defeated the same northern kingdom of Israel with only half as many soldiers as they had because God was with him and intervened in power. Asa also himself when threatened by one million soldiers of the combined Ethiopian and Egyptian armies had simply cried to God and seen the enemy completely destroyed. Yet he now ignores God and His command never to make alliances with the surrounding pagans.

Secondly, he robs the house of God of the very treasures he himself had put into it, in order to bribe the king of Syria to attack his fellow-Israelites.

Thirdly, he had not brought God into his problem, had not trusted the God "whose eyes run to and fro in all the earth to show Himself strong on the behalf of those whose heart is perfect toward Him". Such was the message of the prophet Hanani whom God sent to rebuke the erring king.

Fourthly, the words of God through this prophet indicate that God's real purpose was to humble the Syrian king by means of Asa, whereas by stooping to human schemes "the host of the king of Syria has escaped out of thy hand." Copying the world's ways and philosophies can never be the way to accomplish God's purposes, and in this the prophet drives the message home by saying: "Herein thou hast done foolishly, therefore ... thou shalt have wars". Attacked by Syria, Baasha had been forced to retreat from Ramah, and Asa may have said: "See! It worked!" Scripture shows us that a plan may work and yet be wrong. in which case it is not a move forward but backward. And the seeds were sown for future troubles, for the kings of Syria would from this time be a constant threat. Whatever had happened in Asa's life to undermine his confidence in

God and God's ways we are not told, but we are told that it was a foolish mistake for which he would pay a terrible price.

3. Asa's anger at the messenger of God

Asa's reaction to one sent to point out his mistake was another indication of his spiritual condition (2 Chron 16:10) and it is one which has been demonstrated again and again throughout Scripture both in the Old and New Testaments. Jeroboam behaved similarly to the unnamed prophet from Judah who brought him a message from God. The people of Israel treated Jeremiah in that way when he reminded them of what God's word had taught them; they threw him in a pit and later into a prison from which, to Israel's lasting shame, the pagan Babylonians released him. Ahab and others showed the same bitter attitude. So too did Herod when rebuked by John Baptist. Even Christians can become hostile and threatening under similar circumstances, when they are warned from Scripture about something they are doing.

Asa threw Hanani in prison and proceeded to "oppress some of the people", probably those he saw as supporting the prophet. Three years later the king became "diseased in his feet, until his disease was exceeding great: yet in his disease he sought not to the Lord, but to the physicians". We do not read of restoration in the life of this man who had started out so well and had begun a very promising revival under God, only to nullify it all by disobedience, going to the world for help.

He died two years later, probably as a result of his rotting feet, still refusing to turn to God. He was buried, probably with good reason, in a bed "filled with sweet odours and diverse kinds of spices prepared by the apothecaries." Did he leave poor Hanani in prison? What a sad end for a child of God who could not trust God to do His own work.

Chapter 27

An Abortive Revival under Jehoshaphat

1. Early Stirrings

JEHOSHAPHAT was Asa's son and with the example of his father's failure after a good start before him he might have learned something. Sad to say he seems to have learned nothing for he fell into the same trap of making friends with the wrong people and following their plans for success instead of God's.

The first period of this king's reign showed great promise in every way. Since his father Asa had reigned for forty-one years it is likely that Jehoshaphat was a mature man when he came to the throne and would have had ample opportunity for observing the last disastrous years of that life. This may have inspired him to start off the way he did and it certainly was an impressive beginning, for those first years were all good. It looked as though he would be used of God to bring about the revival which his father had begun but which had ended in ashes.

He seemed above everything else determined to have no dealings with the idolatrous northern kingdom of Israel. In that land the king Baasha who had thrust into Judah and indirectly brought about the spiritual ruin of Asa had died and been succeeded by his son who, after two years was assassinated by Zimri. Zimri, however, only reigned for seven days before being overthrown and with all his family, relatives, and friends completely obliterated (1 Kings 16). Omri who brought this about reigned for twelve years and was followed, three years before Jehoshaphat's coronation, by Ahab, one of the worst kings Israel ever had.

This Ahab had married Jezebel, a Phenician princess from Sidon and a fanatical worshipper of Baal, so Ahab became an ardent convert to this depraved cult and Israel was quickly filled with hundreds of priests and prophets devoted to its practices. All this chaos and corruption probably warned the new king of Judah not only to separate himself entirely from it, but to build strong defences against its intrusion into his own society. In view of what we have already studied about defences, this is important and should be carefully noted. The Judean king, we read in 2 Chron 17, "Strengthened himself against Israel, placed forces in all the fenced cities of Judah, and set garrisons in the land of Judah and in the cities of Ephraim which Asa his father had taken". (Incidentally the occupation of Ephraim, well to the north of the previous border between the two kingdoms, was a very important acquisition, since it formed a broad defensive buffer).

"The Lord was with Jehoshaphat because he walked in the first ways of his father David and sought not unto Baalim; but sought to the Lord God of his father, and walked in His commandments and not after the doings of Israel . . . And his heart was lifted up (encouraged) in the ways of the Lord; moreover he took away the high places and groves out of Judah". All this augured well for the hopes of genuine revival in the nation, and there was more to come.

In the early years of the revival initiated by Asa, though his heart was right before God, the mass of the people were not ready to follow him in his desire to remove the high places at which they were sacrificing to God. Jehoshaphat, perhaps realising that no real return to God can be achieved on a lasting basis without in-depth Bible teaching, set about this very thing, and did so with systematic determination. In the third year of his reign he sent five princes, nine Levites, and two priests "to teach in the cities of Judah" (2 Chron 17:7-9). This would give balance and variety to all the teaching, something best done through different types of teachers rather than a stereotyped one-man-ministry type of arrangement. They apparently did a thorough job and, since a well taught people is the best defence against error and weakness, the nations around took note and "the fear of the Lord fell upon the kingdoms of the land round about Judah". The Philistines even went as far as to send presents and tribute in silver, and the Arabians brought large herds of domestic animals.

2. A Fatal Flaw
a. *Links with Ahab*

This was a high water mark in this revival for from this point we seem to see too great an emphasis on the king's castles (palaces), cities of store, much business, warriors, riches and honour in abundance, in which he "waxed great exceedingly" (2 Chron 17:12 to 18:1). As we have already shown, all of this had been warned against very specifically hundreds of years earlier in Deut 17:16-17. The obtaining of such wealth may have been the first signs of pride and self-satisfaction in this king, as it later marked the decadent church of Laodicea. In the very next sentence of 2 Chron 18 it almost seems as though this prosperity was linked with a growing intimacy with Ahab, or perhaps indicated a desire to be like Ahab. This led to the marrying of his son and heir Jehoram, to Ahab's daughter Athaliah. This woman would follow in her mother's footsteps by developing into a vindictive and reckless murderess. She became Satan's tool who attempted the extermination of all the royal seed of David. Only one baby boy escaped by being hidden from her. On orders from God, Athaliah was expelled and executed on the day the child who survived her slaughter was crowned king in Jerusalem (2 Chron 22:10 through 23). It is the measure of Jehoshaphat's distance from God that he would think of marrying the heir to the throne of David to this pagan Sidonian, who would later try to wipe out his own royal line. This line would be, of course, God's chosen channel for the bringing in of Israel's Messiah, as clearly foretold; hence Satan's antagonism. But there was more to it than this for if we compare the beginning of ch. 17 where Jehoshaphat "strengthened himself against Israel" led by this same Ahab, and the beginning of ch. 18 where Jehoshaphat made affinity with him, we must realise that he was acting against his own knowledge and better judgment. As the story unfolds we see more signs of an uneasy concience.

b. The Character and History of Ahab

In 1 Kings 16:30 wer are told that Ahab did evil in the sight of the Lord above all who were before him. It was because of his wickedness that God sent the famine of the next chapter, but instead of repenting this king tried his best to murder Elijah the prophet who announced the drought. Afterwards the dastardly scheme to murder Naboth so that Ahab could take his vineyard meant Elijah being sent to pronounce a blood-chilling judgment on this murderous pair (1 Kings 21:20-26). And it is after all these things have been recorded that Jehoshaphat king of Judah came down to this wicked king of Israel. It was a sad day for the king, the revival, and Judah.

3. Political and Military Alliance

a. Complex Entanglements

For the visit of the king of Judah to Ahab's court everything was charm and friendliness and for his sake sheep and oxen were killed in abundance. The Hebrew word for "killed" here is used one hundred and forty times in the OT and is almost always rendered as "to sacrifice" or "to offer". So it is highly probable that Ahab was being religiously correct to allay any fears Jehoshaphat might have had. With the ground prepared and as one king to another Ahab now brings up something which obviously he had in mind all along. He asks if Jehoshaphat would go up with him to retake Ramoth-Gilead, though from 1 Kings 22 it seems that he had already discussed this with his servants or counsellors saying; "Ramoth in Gilead is ours" and in

modern language he adds that they are doing nothing
about it. Ramoth-Gilead was one of the six cities of refuge
and was situated on the east side of Jordan. With the
division of the kingdom it formed part of Israel in the
north, belonging to the tribe of Manasseh, so it was not in
any sense the business of the king of Judah. Geographically
it was nearly one hundred miles from Jerusalem, but little
more than forty straight across Jordan from Ahab's capital.
Yet Jehoshaphat's marriage pact with this man may have
included the giving of help in such cases. Perhaps for that
reason the king of Judah found himself in a trap. The
prophet Jehu would put it bluntly in ch. 19 when he said:
"Shouldst thou help the ungodly and love them that hate
the Lord?"

Political theory may have led the king of Judah to take
the course that made him an ally of Ahab. Perhaps he felt
that he could improve his image and add to his strength by
having the power of the northern armies behind him. After
all it has long been a humanistic philosophy that "there is
safety in numbers", and "in numbers is strength", a popular
theme in our day even among Christians. Yet Asa, his
father, had said in prayer when faced by a far greater army
than Syria could ever produce: "it is nothing with thee to
help, whether with many (numbers), or with them that have
no power (might). Help us, O Lord our God, for we rest on
thee and in thy name we go against this multitude". God
had Himself said: "Not by might nor by power, but by my
Spirit, saith the Lord". How oftens this seems to be
forgotten! Asa himself had forgotten this when he sought
the help of Syria, of all peoples, against Israel! Now
everything is turned around and Israel is asking for Judah's
help against Syria. Into such tangles do human schemes
lead us. No wonder Jehoshaphat's revival was on the rocks.

Under Ahab's "persuading" (18:2) the king of Judah says:
"I am as thou art, and my people as thy people; and we will
be with thee in the war." This is the man who, in the first

year of his reign, had "strengthened himself against Israel" over which Ahab was already ruling. The first two statements as to himself and Israel were false, and the last one about joining Ahab in the war was a violation. He knew how different he was from this idolatrous renegade on whom the Lord's curse had already been pronounced because of the blood of Naboth which stained his hands. Indeed if Jehoshaphat could have seen a little ahead he would have known that the sentence of death which had been pronounced by Elijah would be carried out in this very battle against the Syrians. Ahab had already defeated Syria twice, due to the special intervention of God, and one wonders about his keenness to have the king of Judah go with him in full royal regalia while Ahab disguised himself as a common soldier. Did he fear that this might be the end for him, and did he think he could evade the hand of God through this shallow trick? And why would a man who had shown himself as wise and perceptive as Jehoshaphat fall for such an obvious game as this? When we get away from God, or deliberately step outside His revealed will, there is no limit to the folly of which we may be guilty.

b. Lying Prophets

Poor Jehoshaphat! Already requiring to be "persuaded", he now shows himself uncomfortable. Or was he sinking to new depths of hypocrisy, in begging that Ahab might "inquire at the word of the Lord"? Two things are glaringly wrong in this petition.

1. He has already said he would go, and is now committed, so it is a pathetic sham to speak of seeking God's guidance.
2. How did he expect an open idolater and worshipper of Baal to get anything from God who had sentenced him to death (1 Kings 22:28)?

When we leave God's word and follow our own wisdom it is useless to go through the motions of asking Him for guidance or help; we have already turned our backs on His guidance which is always based on His word.

The farce becomes more obvious when Ahab calls up no less than four hundred of his own prophets, who would have to be prophets of Baal. God only needed one, Elijah, to proclaim his truth and overthrow the power of Baal on Mount Carmel, and one, the same Elijah, to pronounce doom on both Ahab and his Jezebel, but apparently in these circles they were impressed by numbers. Of course these false prophets gave a "majority opinion" that the mission would be a success, and numbers carried the day.

c. Micaiah, the Prophet of the Lord

To Jehoshaphat's plaintive request; "Is there not here a prophet of the Lord besides, that we might inquire of him?" Ahab bluntly replies that there is one man, but Ahab hates him "because he never prophesies good to me". One wonders what good any real prophet could possibly find to say to this man, but the king of Judah mildly remarks: "Let not the king say so". They agree to bring Micaiah, and the messenger who is sent to fetch him tries to prompt him to agree with all the other prophets and "let thy word therefore be like one of their's". It is interesting to note that there is no suggestion of calling Elijah but Micaiah was obviously of the same stuff.

It must have been a difficult moment for this servant of God, for the scene was an impressive and daunting one when he finally reached the gathering. The two kings were, we are told, robed and sitting each on his throne in some sort of open square surrouded by four hundred prophets of Baal and probably a great host of other people anxious to witness such an event. One of the prophets, who had decided to dramatise his message with a sort of opening exercise, had made a pair of iron horns and was shouting that with these the two kings would push and consume the king of Syria, while all the others were chanting: "Amen! Go up! Go up!" Honest Micaiah had already said: "What

my God saith, that will I speak", and he now proceeded to
do just that. At first he mocked them by repeating what the
others had been saying, but this was recognised for what it
was and he is adjured (probably by Jehoshaphat, for the
pronoun is singular) that he say nothing but the truth.

The message then comes straight and plain: God had
looked for someone to entice (not persuade as in v. 2) Ahab
to go up and be killed at Ramoth-Gilead and had found this
in the lying prophets. The false prophet with the iron horns
struck Micaiah and the king in fury ordered him to be
taken back to the governor of the city (the word "back"
seems to indicate that he had been in prison before being
called) and fed with "the bread of affliction" until the king
should return in peace.

What a brave man Micaiah was! It is never pleasant to
have to speak out in the face of odds such as he met,
especially when humanly speaking the opposition are in
positions of power and would not hesitate to use that power
to intimidate and coerce. The man who dares to speak
against a powerful majority will likely suffer for it. Joshua
and Caleb were in this threatened minority situation at
Kadesh Barnea, so was Elijah on Mount Carmel, and
Nicodemus in the Sanhedrin, and Paul when before the
governors and kings in Acts 23-26 or when "all they of Asia
turned away from [him]", and so was Luther with his "here
I stand, I can do no other", and Tyndale, and Wesley, and
Whitefield, and many other faithful men including those
who in the nineteenth century came out from the whole
hierarchical ecclesiastical systems of their day to be faithful
to what they found in Holy Scripture. Many of these, not to
mention the many who burned at the stake, paid a high
price for their stand.

It is important to remember that those from the
Reformation down were not standing and suffering for
what would to-day be called "fundamentals" regarding the
deity and humanity of Christ since these were not in
question at that time. They were suffering for the authority

of Scripture as sufficient in itself, and for *church truth* which would liberate them from the bondage of the Roman system and allow them to seek a Biblical pattern for the church. There is a tendency in our day to draw the deity, humanity, and impeccability of Christ (though some would not even include the latter) into a little box and say that if one holds to these two or three doctrines that is all that is needed to be orthodox; the rest is non-fundamental or non-essential, and therefore not important enough to raise questions about. The men we have cited, and many others, would hardly have agreed. They seemed to have a conviction that any of God's truth was worth suffering for, and even dying for. For these truths, including those we mentioned first, the Huguenots were persecuted and scattered far and wide over the world; the Covenanters were hounded over the moors of Scotland by the dragoons of Claverhouse and many of them perished by fire and sword; the Ulster Presbyterians left their homeland in hundreds of thousands in the early seventeen hundreds to seek liberty to practise in North America what they saw as church truth. It has never been easy or popular to stand for truth against a majority.

Having heard the message from the Lord, and seen the messenger insulted and thrown in prison without a word of protest, Jehoshaphat plunged off to Ramoth-Gilead with Ahab, in defiance of the message from God. But the words of the prophet were fulfilled. By a special intervention of God the king of Judah was spared (18:31-32), while a bow drawn, in human eyes by chance, pierced a joint in Ahab's armour. He was driven mortally wounded in his chariot out of the battle and died at sundown. Thus ended this shameful episode which is recorded for our learning.

d. *The Prophet Jehu*

Jehoshaphat, a chastened man, escaped unharmed and made his way back to Jerusalem where he was met by the prophet Jehu who, without mincing words brought his sinful mistake home to him. We have already given some of the words of this message but it is so important that it should all be given at this point. 2 Chron 19:2-3 reads as follows: "Shouldest thou help the ungodly, and love them that hate the Lord? Therefore there is wrath upon thee from the Lord. Nevertheless there are good things found in thee in that thou hast taken away the groves (*asherah*) out of the land, and hast prepared thy heart to seek the Lord. And Jehoshaphat dwelt in Jerusalem, and went out again through the people from Beer-Sheba to Mount Ephraim, and brought them back to the Lord God of their fathers." This would indicate that the king had listened to the word of God, had humbled himself and been restored to fellowship with the Lord. He even set about cleaning up the judical system (19:5-11) and making sure that the right men were running it. Then a great army of Ammonites and Moabites came against Judah and got as far as Engedi, a mere twenty-five miles south east of Jerusalem. But the king led his people to seek help from God instead of trying in his own strength, and the enemy was completely defeated.

4. A Further Alliance with the King of Israel

Nevertheless national revival was stopped short and a number of things haunt one in considering the whole course of this man and the great revival which began with such promise, stalled and never seemed to get going again. His erratic character which shows up in his going forward then backward; building defences against the northern kingdom then entering into marriage, social, and military alliances with it; seeming to repent and to have learned his lesson and then falling into almost the same trap again; asking for a "prophet of the Lord" to obtain God's guidance about his alliance with Ahab, and then ignoring the message when it was given; his staggering gullibility in the matter of going into battle in full royal regalia while Ahab went disguised as a common soldier. God in grace records the fact that he did what was right in the sight of the Lord, no doubt meaning that his intentions were good and he accomplished much for God, yet his shocking inconsistency even in his well-doing is faithfully written for our instruction and warning.

Some, through careless reading think of 1 Kings 22: 48-49 and 2 Chron 20:35-36 as records of the same incident. Some critics actually use them to prove that there are mistakes in the Bible! For the following reasons it is clear that two incidents are referred to:

1. In Kings "Tarshish-ships", referring to a type of ship or rigging, were built to go to Ophir for gold. There is no certainty as to where Ophir is but because of its products all encyclopaedists and commentators deduce that it was south or east of Israel. Guesses range from the Arabian Peninsula to East Africa and even Indian.

2. In Chronicles ships of an unspecified type are built to go to Tarshish. Because Jonahs attempted voyage to that port took him west on the Mediterranean, and for many other reasons, this port is commonly believed to have been in Spain. In any case it is obviously *not* Ophir.

In Kings we are told that Ahaziah son of Ahab, by this time reigning in Israel, proposed a joint business venture which was rejected by the King of Judah. On the contrary we are told in Chronicles that Jehoshaphat joined with Ahaziah "to make the ships to go to Tarshish." In this passage the prophet Eliezer rebuked the king for joining himself with the wicked king of Israel. In both instances the trading venture never took place and the ships were "broken" at Ezion-geber.

It would seem that the Kings passage refers to the earlier of the two incidents, and if this is so the king of Judah was then wise enough to turn down any alliance with the wicked Ahaziah, son of Jezebel. If this sequence is accepted then he later changed his mind, or broke down, and entered into a partnership he had first properly rejected. Whatever way it is considered it is a sad story, and the more so since in both books it is recorded after Jehoshaphat's death and therefore appears to be a retrospective glance at a weakness in the man. There is much to be learned from all this in relation to our own day, for these things were "written for our admonition" (1 Cor 10:11).

Chapter 28

An Abortive Revival under Joash

1. Early Influences

THIS Joash, who in the book of the Kings is called Jehoash, was in his early life one of the most dramatic and beautiful characters of the OT (see 2 Kings 11-13; 2 Chron 23, 24). The days were dark, for Athaliah, daughter of Ahab and Jezebel, whom Jehoshaphat had married to his son in defiance of God's prohibition, had slaughtered every remaining royal heir of David, except one who was hidden and who was this Joash. She then reigned over Judah as a usurper for six years while her sons built a temple to Baal and looted God's temple to enrich their blasphemous house of abominations. Joash was crowned king when he was seven years old, and immediately, under the guidance of his uncle the high priest, began a restoration of the temple and took the first steps toward revival.

Athaliah was executed on orders from God and Jehoiada the high priest had started this movement by making a covenant "between . . . all the people and . . . the king that they should be the Lord's people". This last phrase is a striking one and (we believe) this is the first time it is used in this way. It was a good start.

It is clear, however, that many of the first steps were initiated by the high priest rather than by the king, though we read that "Joash was minded to repair the house of the Lord", indicating that he had a heart for God's dwelling place. Jehoiada's name appears again and again in the early part of the young king's life, leading him surely in the right direction. It seemed as though a new bright day of restoration was dawning with great promise.

174

2. The Signs of Defection
a. The Pressure of the Princes

We soon note, however, a rather ominous hint of trouble in the words, "Joash did right in the sight of the Lord all the days of Jehoiada the priest", and that they "offered burnt offerings in the house of the Lord continually" throughout that godly man's life. However, we read in 2 Chron 24:15 that Jehoiada died "full of days being one hundred and thirty years old" and he was given the unique honour of being "buried in the city of David among the kings because he had done good in Israel, both toward God and toward His house".

Immediately the princes of Judah, perhaps jealous and resenting the influence of this priest of the tribe of Levi over the scion of David king of Judah, came before him "and the king hearkened unto them". It now becomes evident that while Joash had moved with the tide of revival the real impetus came from the priest rather than the king, and with the restraint of Jehoiada removed the king allowed himself to be swept back by the power of these popular princes of royal blood. They left the house of the Lord and began again to worship the *Asherah* and other idols, until God's patience ran out. Yet he sent prophets to warn them of the end of this road under the anger of God, but they would not listen.

b. The Courage of a Prophet

One of the most outstanding of these prophets was Zechariah the son of Jehoiada, therefore the king's own cousin, who bravely stood against the tide of new people who were leading the nation astray, and rebuked them. But the people stoned the brave man to death "at the commandment of the king in the court of the house of the Lord" and silenced the lone voice to be heard in the whole land (2 Chron 24:20-21). The Holy Spirit adds that in doing this "the king remembered not the kindness which Jehoiada his father had done him" and in dying the prophet cried,

"Lord, look upon it and require it". In Matt 23:35 the Lord Himself reminded the Jews who were about to crucify Him that this blood of Zechariah would come on them in judgment.

c. Divine Retribution

That same year the Syrians came "with a very small company of men", but because of the sin of His people it was enough for God's purpose and Judah was severely defeated, while the invaders "destroyed all the princes from among the people, and sent the spoil to the king of Damascus ... because they had forsaken the Lord God of their fathers". They left Joash behind them "in great diseases" or as some translators have it have it "severely wounded", but his own servants "slew [him] on his bed, and he died."

What are we to learn from this disaster? At least this: that it is not enough simply to follow others in a wave of revival if our own heart is not in it, and our spirit is not broken and contrite before God. It also shows us how fatal it is to follow the crowd who profess to show us a better way which may not be God's way. May we heed the warning of such an example. We must beware of popular princes who would woo us with attractive schemes to win people, even though it be at the cost of following the gods of the age. Joash did this very thing, once free from the wise direction of the priestly man of God, full of days and the wisdom of the Lord.

Chapter 29

Conclusions

HAVING studied the case histories of five great Biblical revivals, we must now look back and ask ourselves if we have found a common pattern. Are there some solutions, some basic principles, which would serve as a guide in our search for a much needed restoration of God's power and presence among us? That we are in sore need of such reviving there can be no doubt, and many are concerned and burdened, even distressed, and agonising about our general condition. This condition has several manifestations. In some cases it is a deadness, a featureless inertia, a lack of thought and care for the lost around us, and a lack of intelligent worship or true heart devotion to the Lord. It may also appear as a ritualistic attendance at meetings and services while lives and energies are given over to worldly ways of thinking, materialism, money-making, success, sport and all the other attractions of the self-centred society in which we live. It may even be expressed in the "churchiness" of the religious world, whether in its sedate, solemn, and somnolent imitation of the paced ritualism of the establishment, or the more lively style of the televangelists with all the emphasis on bright programming, lots of entertainment, music, and achieving the goal of big numbers.

With the awareness of our need has come a torrent of books, articles, conferences, seminars, counsellors, church consultants, and "how-to" sessions. Alas! Very few if any of these get to the heart of the matter, for neither numbers, size, nor success as measured by the religious world's standards is the cure for our malady, which is a deeply-spiritual one, of the heart and the inner life and affections of the soul. We could put into operation almost any of the proffered solutions and gain more people and yet our own spiritual condition be no better. What does it profit us to have an auditorium filled for every service and our church numbers growing weekly if this is not the result of genuine conversions following conviction of sin and repentance toward God? This is exactly where most of the mainline denominations have wound up, to say nothing of some extremely large church organisations that have been exposed as rotten with greed, pride, downright dishonesty, and moral dirt while the numbers continued to grow. We are wearied with this and cry out longingly to God for a deeply spiritual awakening as distinct from mere numerical success.

It is the thesis of this little book that in the Biblical revivals whose course we have been tracing we have indeed found these very things we need, flowing from a coming back to the Holy Scripture and being convicted by its study of disobedience to its basic precepts or, which is as bad, ignorance of them. Whether in the times of Joshua, Samuel, Hezekiah, Josiah, or Ezra the story is the same. There is a sense of departure, of failure, and sin which is confessed. In Samuel's days we read that Israel "lamented after the Lord", not after success, numbers, or even blessing, important though these may be, but after God Himself and a sense of His presence which they had so sadly lost. In the days of Josiah the book is rediscovered and this book brings home to them a deep consciousness of having departed from God and transgressed His commands and teachings. Ezra "brings the book" and it touches and penetrates hearts, bringing about a real return to the Lord. This is revival as distinguished from restructuring, reprogramming, or brightening up services and getting more people into them. We badly need a rediscovery of the Book.

We have found also, we believe, much to sover us in the consideration of the revivals which began well but died through very serious mistakes. In the case of Asa this was through turning to the arm of the flesh instead of to God. In Jehoshaphat it was by thinking that he could further his programme for enhancing the nation by adopting the political schemes of the world of his day and entering into alliance with his deadliest enemy. In Joash it was by not only abandoning the wisdom of his revered and spiritually-experienced mentor, but turning to the noble, and no doubt younger, princes of Judah who were to lead him into disaster and themselves into destruction.

May God give us humble hearts to learn from these things, and true obedience in subjection to His holy word.